ATD Soft Skills Series

Teamwork
in Talent Development

Thane Bellomo

PRESS

Alexandria, VA

ATD Press is an internationally renowned source of insightful and practical information on talent development, training, and professional development.

ATD Press
1640 King Street
Alexandria, VA 22314 USA

Ordering information: Books published by ATD Press can be purchased by visiting ATD's website at td.org/books or by calling 800.628.2783 or 703.683.8100.

Library of Congress Control Number: 2021939796

ISBN-10: 1-952157-66-8
ISBN-13: 978-1-952157-66-0
e-ISBN: 978-1-952157-67-7

ATD Press Editorial Staff
Director: Sarah Halgas
Manager: Melissa Jones
Content Manager, Career Development: Lisa Spinelli
Developmental Editor: Jack Harlow
Production Editor: Hannah Sternberg
Text Design: Shirley E.M. Raybuck
Cover Design: John Anderson Jr.

Printed by BR Printers, San Jose, CA

To my Mom and Dad,
who always believe in me.

To Seth Beardsley and Brian Zukauckas
for their thought partnership.

To my children Calvin, Charlie, Sam, and Coco,
who have taught me what matters.

Contents

About the Series

The world of work is changing. As companies once prioritized radical workplace performance and productivity improvements, they focused on training their employees with the purpose of getting more work done faster. But companies have learned that while their people might be increasingly productive, they aren't working better, particularly with each other. Lurking on the horizon is always greater automation, which will continue to shift the balance between the needs for hard and soft skills. Employees of the future will spend more time on activities that machines are less capable of, such as managing people, applying expertise, and communicating with others. More than ever, soft skills are being recognized as a premium.

Enter talent development.

TD professionals play a unique role in addressing the increasing demand for soft skills. They work with people and on behalf of people: A trainer facilitating a group of learners. A team of instructional designers working cross-functionally to address a business need. A learning manager using influence to make the case for increased budget or resources. But how can TD professionals expect to develop future employees in these soft skills if they're not developing their own?

At the Association for Talent Development (ATD), we're dedicated to creating a world that works better and empowering TD professionals like you to develop talent in the workplace. As part of this effort, ATD developed the Talent Development Capability Model, a framework to guide the TD profession in what practitioners need to know and do to develop themselves, others, and their organizations. While soft skills appear most prominently under the Building Personal Capability domain, these crucial skills cross every capability in the model, including those under Developing Professional Capability and Impacting Organizational Capability. Soft skills enable TD professionals to take their instructional design, training delivery and facilitation, future readiness, change management, and other TD capabilities to the next level.

Just as TD professionals need resources on how to develop talent, they need guidance in improving their interpersonal and intrapersonal skills—to be more adaptable, self-aware and empathetic, creative, team-oriented and collaborative, and influential and persuasive. This ATD series provides such guidance.

Organized with two parts, each book in the ATD Soft Skills Series tackles one soft skill that TD professionals need to foster in themselves to help the people and organizations they serve. Part 1 breaks down the skill into what it is, why it's important, and the internal or external barriers to improving it. Part 2 turns the lens on the daily work of TD professionals and how they can practice and perfect that skill on the job. Featuring worksheets, self-reflection exercises, and best practices, these books will empower TD professionals to build career resiliency by matching their technical expertise with newfound soft skill abilities.

Books in the series:
- *Adaptability in Talent Development*
- *Emotional Intelligence in Talent Development*
- *Creativity in Talent Development*
- *Teamwork in Talent Development*
- *Influence in Talent Development*

We're happy to bring you the ATD Soft Skills Series and hope these books support you in your future learning and development.

Jack Harlow, Series Editor
Senior Developmental Editor, ATD Press

Series Foreword

Oh, Those Misnamed Soft Skills!

For years organizations have ignored soft skills and emphasized technical skills, often underestimating the value of working as a team, communicating effectively, using problem solving skills, and managing conflict. New managers have failed because their promotions are often based on technical qualifications rather than the soft skills that foster relationships and encourage teamwork. Trainers as recently as a dozen years ago were reluctant to say that they facilitated soft skills training. Why?

Soft Skills: The Past and Now

The reluctance to admit to delivering (or requiring) soft skills often starts with the unfortunate name, "soft," which causes people to view them as less valuable than "hard" skills such as accounting or engineering. The name suggests they are easy to master or too squishy to prioritize developing. On both counts that's wrong. They aren't. In fact, Seth Godin calls them "real" skills, as in, "Real because they work, because they're at the heart of what we need today" (Godin 2017).

Yet, as a society, we seem to value technical skills over interpersonal skills. We tend to admire the scientists who discovered the vaccine for COVID-19 over leaders who used their communication skills to engage the workforce when they were quarantined at home. We easily admit to not knowing how to fly an airplane but readily believe we are creative or can adapt on the fly. We think that because we've been listening all our lives, we are proficient at it—when we're not. As a result, we put much more emphasis on developing our technical skills through advanced degrees and post–higher education training or certifications to land that first or next job than we do on mastering our interpersonal and intrapersonal skills.

Fortunately, many businesses and their leaders are now recognizing the value of having a workforce that has technical knowledge supported by soft skills. That's good because soft skills matter more to your career than you may envision. Consider: as a part of the Jobs Reset Summit, the World Economic Forum determined that 50 percent of the workforce needed reskilling and upskilling. The summit also identified the top 10 job reskilling needs for the future. Eight of the 10 required skills in the 21st century are nontechnical; these skills include creativity, originality, and initiative; leadership and social influence; and resilience, stress tolerance, and flexibility (Whiting 2020). LinkedIn's 2019 *Global Talent Trends Report* showed that acquiring soft skills is the most important trend fueling the future of the workplace: 91 percent of the respondents said that soft skills matter as much or more than technical skills and 80 percent believed they were critical to organizational success (Chandler 2019). A Deloitte report (2017) suggested that "soft skill–intensive occupations will account for two-thirds of all jobs by 2030" and that employees who practice skills associated with collaboration, teamwork, and innovation may be worth $2,000 more per year to businesses. As the cost of robots decreases and AI improves, soft skills like teamwork, problem solving, creativity, and influence will become more important.

Soft skills may not be as optional as one might originally imagine.

Soft Skills: Their Importance

Soft skills are sometimes referred to as enterprise skills or employability skills. Despite their bad rap, they are particularly valuable because they are transferable between jobs, careers, departments, and even industries, unlike hard or technical skills, which are usually relevant only to specific jobs. Communication often lands at the top of the soft skill list, but the category encompasses other skills, such as those included in the ATD Soft Skills Series: emotional intelligence, adaptability, teamwork, creativity, and influence. These personal attributes influence how well employees build trust, establish accountability, and demonstrate professional ethics.

Soft skills are also important because almost every job requires employees to interact with others. Organizations require a workforce that has technical skills and formal qualifications for each job; however, the truth is that business is about relationships. And, organizations depend on relationships to be successful. This is where successful employees, productive organizations, and soft skills collide.

Soft Skills and the Talent Development Capability Model

Talent development professionals are essential links to ensure that organizations have all the technical and soft skills that are required for success. I sometimes get exhausted just thinking about everything we need to know to ensure success for our organizations, customers, leaders, learners, and ourselves. The TD profession is no cookie-cutter job. Every day is different; every design is different; every delivery is different; and every participant is different. We are lucky to have these differences because these broad requirements challenge us to grow and develop.

As TD professionals, we've always known that soft skills are critical for the workforce we're responsible for training and developing. But what about yourself as a TD professional? What soft skills do you require to be effective and successful in your career? Have you ever thought about all the skills in which you need to be proficient?

ATD's Talent Development Capability Model helps you define what technical skills you need to improve, but you need to look beyond the short capability statements to understand the soft skills required to support each (you can find the complete model on page 48). Let's examine a few examples where soft skills are required in each of the domains.

- **Building Personal Capability** is dedicated to soft skills, although all soft skills may not be called out. It's clear that communication, emotional intelligence, decision making, collaboration, cultural awareness, ethical behavior, and lifelong learning are soft skills.

Project management may be more technical, but you can't have a successful project without great communication and teamwork.

- **Developing Professional Capability** requires soft skills throughout. Could instructional design, delivery, and facilitation exist without creativity? You can't coach or attend to career development without paying attention to emotional intelligence (EI) and influence. Even technology application and knowledge management require TD professionals to be adaptable, creative, and team players for success.

- **Impacting Organizational Capability** focuses on the soft skills you'll use while working at the leadership and organizational level. For you to have business insight, be a partner with management, and develop organizational culture, you will need to build teamwork with the C-suite, practice influencing, and use your EI skills to communicate with them. Working on a talent strategy will require adaptability and influence. And you can't have successful change without excellent communication, EI, and teamwork. Future readiness is going to require creativity and innovation.

Simply put, soft skills are the attributes that enable TD professionals to interact effectively with others to achieve the 23 capabilities that span the spectrum of disciplines in the Capability Model.

Soft Skills: The Key to Professionalism

So, as TD professionals we need to be proficient in almost all soft skills to fulfill the most basic responsibilities of the job. However, there's something even more foundational to the importance of developing our soft skills: Only once we've mastered these skills can we project the professionalism that will garner respect from our stakeholders, our learners, and our peers. We must be *professional,* or why else are we called *TD professionals?*

Professionalism is the driving force to advance our careers. To earn the title of TD professional we need to be high performers and exhibit the qualities and skills that go beyond the list of technical TD skills. We need to be soft-skill proficient to deliver services with aplomb. We need to be team members to demonstrate we work well with others. We need to be EI-fluent to ensure that we are aware of, control, and express our emotions and handle interpersonal relationships well. We need to be creative to help our organization achieve a competitive advantage. We need to be adaptable to future-proof our organizations. And we need influencing skills that help us earn that proverbial seat at the table.

We all need role-specific knowledge and skills to perform our jobs, but those who achieve the most are also proficient in soft skills. You will use these skills every day of your life, in just about every interaction you have with others. Soft skills allow you to demonstrate flexibility, resourcefulness, and resilience—and as a result, enhance your professionalism and ensure career success. And a lack of them may just limit your career potential.

Clearly, soft skills are more critical than once thought and for TD professionals and trainers they are likely to be even more critical. Your participants and customers expect you to be on the leading edge of most topics that you deliver. And they also expect you to model the skills required for a successful career. So, which soft skills do you need to become a *professional* TD professional? Is it clearer communication? Interpersonal savvy? Increased flexibility? Self-management? Professional presence? Resourcefulness?

E.E. Cummings said, "It takes courage to grow up and become who you really are." I hope that you have the courage to determine which skills you need to improve to be the best trainer you can be—and especially to identify those misnamed soft skills that aren't *soft* at all. Then establish standards for yourself that are high enough to keep you on your training toes. The five books in the ATD Soft Skills Series offer you a great place to start.

Elaine Biech, Author
Skills for Career Success: Maximizing Your Potential at Work

Introduction

The wind-swept hills of southeast Turkey are arid. Fertile valleys give way to dry hills dotted with shrubs and small trees. Small villages populate the green valleys and goat farmers have eked out a living in these hills for thousands of years. There is nothing here to suggest anything other than the slow passage of time. And yet, in 1994, on a small hill roughly translated as Pot Belly Hill, Klaus Schmidt of the German Archaeological Institute began to fully explore Gobekli Tepe. You may not have heard of Gobekli Tepe (not many people have), but among the many fascinating things there are to know about it, it may also be one of the most important landmarks in the history of teamwork.

Gobekli Tepe is huge. Across a dozen acres, it is a buried complex of stone monuments and structures. Enormous monoliths standing more than 20 feet tall with intricate relief carvings are arranged in geometric order and weigh up to 20 tons. The complex was apparently built over centuries by the people of this land. Archeologists presume it was a temple structure of some kind, but we cannot be sure why so many hundreds or thousands of people would labor consistently over centuries to build such a place. Indeed, the scope of the Gobekli Tepe cannot be overstated in its complexity, the logistical coordination required to build it, and the engineering knowledge applied to complete such a massive undertaking.

What makes the complex so incredibly extraordinary, almost impossible even, is that it was built more than 11,000 years ago. You read that correctly—11,000 years. That is more than 5,000 years before the Great Pyramids. Its construction was so far back into the dawn of precivilization that it was built during a time when archeologists have presumed that humans were merely small bands of hunters and gatherers living in caves and scrubbing the forests and hills for food and shelter. How is this possible, you might ask? By what miracle did these ancient hunters and gatherers band together to labor for centuries to create such a wonder of the world? We do not know, and we may never know. But we do know that for whatever reason they labored together over many centuries, and that reason was important to them. The importance of the work inspired and motivated these people to use their natural predisposition to collaborate and cooperate to dedicate generations of effort to accomplishing a monumental task.

Teamwork Is Human Nature

I tell this story because Gobekli Tepe demonstrates the power of collaboration and teamwork on a scale almost unimaginable. What it took to mine and carve 25-ton granite blocks, transport them, design and build the complex structures, and coordinate hundreds (if not thousands) of people and provide food, water, and shelter is almost beyond imagination for the presumably "primitive" nature of these small hunter-gatherer groups. And the skills required to accomplish such an undertaking did not appear overnight.

The discovery of Gobekli Tepe most certainly reaffirms not only the power of teamwork, but also that humans are the inheritors of a primal instinct to work together, to collaborate, and to coordinate to accomplish important work. We are wired to work together in the same way that wolves hunt in packs or trees grow in fertile soil; it is simply what humans do. In fact, there was never a time when people didn't work together. There was never a first time when two people got together and decided, "You know what, we should work together!" No, the power of teamwork resides within every one of us. If hunter-gatherers more than 11,000 years ago could come together to build such things, surely we are capable of the same. As we go forward together to explore teams and teamwork, keep the story of Gobekli Tepe in mind.

Over thousands of years of incremental cooperation and collaboration, we have succeeded in building the world we live in today. Working together allowed us to build functioning societies, raise families, live in ordered communities, and run organizations. And that, in the end, is the point of this book. How can we most effectively leverage this innate sense of teaming to accomplish important things that we've used for millennia? How can we most effectively identify, develop, and hone this teaming predisposition into a set of processes and, most importantly, skills that we can get better at? How can we use this predisposition to work together to improve our teams and our organizations and to potentially continue to help your organization and indeed humanity on its journey?

You may smirk at the notion that you are engaged in helping humanity itself achieve something. You are, perhaps, only a small cog in a large mechanism. Maybe you are a talent development consultant or an L&D professional. Perhaps you are a leader running a small or even large organization. It may feel like your contribution to such a large story is necessarily small; minute even. But I am here to assure you that the contribution you are capable of making is not insignificant. Humanity progresses in incremental fashion. As you lead or contribute to your teams, you are presumably accomplishing something; something useful and important to whatever it is you and your organization do. And all those tiny accomplishments add up to something that has the potential to be a force for good in the world, to your organization, to your teammates, and to yourself.

The Power of Teams

Teams are powerful. Fundamentally, the team is the unit whereby change in our organizations happens. It is in the collaboration of ideas and the sharing of perspectives that allows us to accomplish something meaningful. It is in this struggle that people grow and develop into something more than they were before. And we can thus contribute to our shared endeavor more powerfully than we previously could.

Great good can come from teams that goes far beyond the output the team has been tasked to create. The sense of purpose, community, and belonging that great teams generate is the most powerful force for loyalty and engagement your organization can leverage. Of course, it may be that your organizational mission is so compelling that people will dedicate their lives to whatever it is you do based on the honor of working for you. But more than likely, people's loyalties are rooted in the people that they work, live, and breathe with each day. This dedication to one another and to the mission of the team translates into organizational dedication and discretionary effort that can reach far beyond the confines of that individual team. It has the power to create intrinsic motivations that generate activity not for money, power, or prestige, but because they are in the service of the goal and each other.

Therefore, let us also not forget, as we sometimes do, that our participation in collectively accomplishing something important not only helps our organization, but it also has the potential to have a profound impact on each of us. Our experience working on teams is the venue where many of us get the most satisfaction from our work. It is the vehicle where we can most effectively see our efforts bear fruit. It can help us see that we have something to contribute. In the crucible of struggle within a real team doing important work, all our strengths and weaknesses become apparent. In that context, teams can help us understand that what we can offer, and indeed who we are, is not only good enough but is valuable.

If You Want Teamwork, Give the Team Work

Important work is the catalyzing force that prompts people to display the attributes of high-performing teams: engagement, discretionary effort, curiosity, challenge-seeking, accountability, the development of trust and vulnerability, and the creation of community and belonging. Without important work, we generally see none of these things; in fact, the inverse is true. When people engage in unimportant work, they commonly display attributes that we associate with poor teams: disengagement, apathy, little discretionary effort, low accountability, and mistrust. When people engage in work that is important to them, they gravitate toward its accomplishment because of that importance. They are willing to endure suffering, they are eager to engage, and they are forced by the hardship of that effort to bring their true selves to the team. And it is in the sharing of this common experience that trust, community, belonging, and acceptance come to them, creating a virtuous cycle that powers true teams to accomplish things they may not have thought possible.

All of this is nothing to diminish. How we organize our teams, how we lead our teams, and how we participate in our teams has a real impact on people. When done well, teams have the power to engage and validate. But they also have the power to disengage and invalidate. Teams can reshape your organization and its people. Using teams wisely and effectively can take your organization to another level and elevate its members in many ways. Used unwisely, teams can disengage employees, ruin your culture, and sow mistrust. Provide people with excellent team leadership in accomplishing important and difficult work, and your team will likely perform well. Present people with unimportant work and poor leadership, and they will likely perform poorly—no matter how many team-building exercises you have. When creating a team, it is important to think deeply about its implications; for you, your organization, and the members of your team.

How This Book Will Help You
The burden of team leadership is heavier than we might otherwise think. Talent development professionals play a significant role in addressing team effectiveness. While leaders are the ones who actually lead teams, they are sometimes ill-equipped to understand team dynamics. They are primarily the ones who throw people together to solve a problem without thinking much about how to best craft the team to gain all the secondary benefits that we will talk about. Talent development professionals can encourage

leaders to take appropriate action. They can influence leaders on how to best create the conditions whereby the team will develop the kind of dedication to each other that will harvest the most value.

To fulfill this critical function, talent development professionals must understand the circumstances whereby great teams emerge, as well as the leadership skills and decision points that foster great teams. But before they can do that, they must develop their own teamwork skills. Because while we are primed to collaborate and cooperate to accomplish things, that doesn't necessarily mean we are naturally very good at it. Teamwork is a skill like any other, and we can get better at it.

With this in mind, this book is for leaders, TD professionals serving as team leaders, and team members who wish to build great teams and improve their team performance. That said, the contents, approaches, and methodologies are applicable to any team in any industry. Teams and how to best think about them are as universal as any characteristic that humans exhibit.

We start by defining teams and teamwork in chapter 1. In chapters 2 and 3 we will talk about why teams are important and some of the challenges related to teaming and how to overcome them. In chapter 4 we will discuss why teamwork matters so much for talent development professionals and their work, with a look at how teamwork ties into the capabilities for successful talent development. We will also introduce a model for how best to think about teamwork that maps team skills and the progression from the establishment of important work and clear goals (chapter 5) through the development of a curiosity and challenge culture (chapters 6 and 7). In chapters 8 and 9 we discuss how these attributes, when done well, ultimately lead to the kind of trust and community that will help power your organization in ways you may not have thought possible.

It is my hope that you will walk away from reading this book with a newfound appreciation for not only the importance of teaming, but also how you and your organization can get better at it to drive greater levels of engagement, innovation, and community. I hope that you will build a deeper understanding of how organizations can most effectively leverage the most powerful tool that humanity has at its disposal to move your organization forward to accomplish great things.

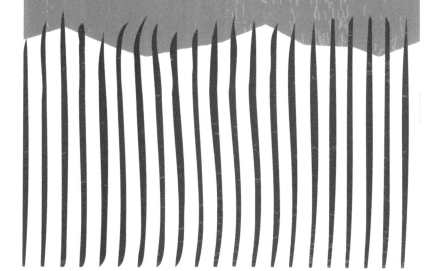

PART 1

Making the Case for Teamwork

CHAPTER 1

What Is Teamwork?

You've probably been on a number of teams in your life. Sports teams are where many of us had our first opportunity to experience what it is like to be on a team. Working with groups in a religious organization, school, or community are other places where we may have been introduced to the idea of teaming. These experiences often shape our initial understanding of what it is like to collaborate, coordinate, and cooperate. They give us a pretty decent understanding of what it is like to work together to accomplish something.

Through those experiences we also get to see what success in teaming looks and feels like . . . and also what it's like to work with ineffective groups. If you are like me, you found some of those experiences to be satisfying and others to be much less so. As I think back on those early experiences, I find myself chuckling at the mess some of them were, such as the school fundraiser that was semi-organized by the two energetic parents and "supported" by a dozen others who showed up on the final day to "help." All of them may have called themselves teams at some point or another, but many most assuredly were not.

Commonly defined, a team is the group of individuals working together to achieve their goal, and teamwork is the collaborative effort of the group to achieve that common goal in the most effective and efficient way.

Fair enough. However, I would define a team a little differently. In my years of consulting with dozens of organizations and hundreds of leaders, I have noticed a distinct difference in outcomes between what I would call a team versus a group of people doing things together. So when people ask me what a team is, my answer is:

> A group of people working together to accomplish an important goal, as understood by the team, that requires the efforts of each team member to successfully accomplish.

When these components are present, the benefits of teaming can be realized: community, purpose, trust, and engagement. When they are not, we may get things accomplished, but the broader benefits of teaming will not manifest themselves. This is fundamentally what this book is about: How you can leverage teams to get important things done but also to build the connections and community that generate the loyalties driving broad organizational engagement. And, most importantly, you must understand that all of these things are learned behaviors—skills that can be developed. As we will see, the modern workplace requires the development of this skill set. Teams are the primary units of production in almost all areas of work, and organizations lacking in understanding of how teams form and function will be at a disadvantage.

It's important to be on the same page on what a team is. One thing I have learned over the years is that when we call something a "team" when it is not, we are disappointed when we do not see the ancillary benefits that we would expect from a team. I have seen work groups or professional practices continually work on their team because they aren't seeing the benefits of camaraderie, shared values and norms, and constructive conflict that good teams generate. Their frustration is understandable.

As an example, I once worked with a group of organization development (OD) professionals who desperately wanted to be a team. They all worked in the same department, they all did the same kind of work, and they all reported to the same leader. But they all had different clients who had different priorities, they worked together rarely, and they had no common goal. They were an OD practice, but not a team. But they were disappointed that they didn't have the kind of closeness and affinity they thought a team should have. They didn't really have the same aspirations, values, shared beliefs, and personal bonds they thought being on a team would bring. Deep down, they wanted those things. This is not uncommon.

Human beings are, after all, social animals. We need connection. We need to belong. We need to feel valued. We need to love and be loved. People get these things from all kinds of places: their families, their religious affiliations, their civic and community organizations. But many of us spend a lot of time—a substantial portion of our lives—at our jobs, and it is not weird that we want to experience a sense of community in our places of employment. Teaming in the workplace is directly connected to these secondary benefits and the powerful impact they can have on the larger organization. This is a theme we will return to time and again throughout this book: the idea that true teams and teaming get a lot of stuff done, but also create benefits that extend well beyond the team and have the power to transform your organization for the better. But to garner these benefits, we must focus our efforts on actual teams rather than workgroups.

Are You a Team or Workgroup?

Think of a time when you were voluntold to be in a group where you had to accomplish some body of work that you and everyone else on the team knew wasn't all that important. We have all been there before. It often needs to be done, but we can't say the task is all that fun or meaningful. We enter into such work with a sense of resignation and do our best to engage so that we can get it over with as quickly as possible. Contrast that with times you have been on real teams where the work you were engaged in was actually important, and the group had the visceral sense that it was. The feeling is very different. The group is energized by the work and eager to get started. The difference between these two groups is not the people or the leader, but rather the work itself. The latter group has the possibility to become a high-performing team. The first group generally does not.

We have all been on workgroups. We have all experienced the dynamic of people only intermittently providing their best work, weak enthusiasm, and variable participation, and a few people shouldering most of the burden. It may be that the actual work the group is trying to accomplish isn't that important, and they know it. Maybe it is just busy work that needs to be completed. Maybe the work is what I call brand management, or work done solely to demonstrate that we are here and we are working.

If the work isn't actually important, recognize that it isn't and thus you are not going to get the broader benefits of a team. You should be honest with yourself and your people about this. We all recognize that we sometimes have to do work that is unimportant. Being dishonest about it and trying to sell something unimportant as important just diminishes trust. It sets people up to be skeptical when you do have important work to do.

Important work thus defines the team, and not all work is important. While that should seem obvious, many leaders reflexively think all work is important. Or they don't recognize that really important work requires thinking purposefully about more than just what bodies can we put on the team. If it is important work and you decide you are going to create a real team, then leaders need to consider what expertise they need on the team and what personalities and perspectives will give the team a diverse enough perspective so that the outcome will be as successful as it can be. Who needs the kind of development that being on the team might provide? Who is interested in the work? Who needs to be mentored through the work, and who can do the mentoring?

When done well, being on a team can provide not only the pride of creating the tangible outputs the team was charged with producing, but also a sense of belonging and engagement, common norms and values, and the generation of innovative solutions. We will use our definition of a team as we go forward to ensure that we are not confusing teams with workgroups.

The role of talent development professionals in this capacity is pretty clear. You should influence and coach leaders to define the importance of the work, clarify whether they want to create a team or a workgroup, and determine how to craft the team in a way that will be most effective to not only get the work done, but also create and leverage the secondary benefits of teaming. You should also work closely with leaders to gain clarity and commitment on what autonomy the team will have, what values it will embrace as it moves forward, and what problem the team is trying to solve. And for those talent development departments, it means practicing this idea within your own team and demonstrating the difference to the greater organization. Going forward, we will explore all of these teaming components.

 Consider This

- A team is a group of people working together toward an important goal that requires the efforts of every member to achieve. The importance of the work defines the team.
- Be honest about the motivation for the work and the reasons for it.
- When leading a team, do the upfront work of purposefully thinking through whether you want to create a team or a workgroup. Delineating the importance of the work is the first step in this process. Decide whether the work is important and whether you are prepared to support that work by giving the team sufficient autonomy, funding, and ability to problem solve.

The Myth of the Loner

Not much that will broadly impact the organization gets done by individuals anymore. Gone are the days when someone working alone late into the evening will create and implement a solution to a broad organizational problem. Organizations are too sub-specialized and dispersed to easily allow individuals to move the organization in one direction or another.

In fact, the individual may not have ever really done so. This has been written about extensively before, but it is worth mentioning. The classic example is the inventor Thomas Edison. Much has been made of his individual brilliance in inventing the light bulb, the movie camera, and so on. But it is worth noting that he had a team of technicians and scientists at

Menlo Park that co-created many of these inventions. For example, it was William Kennedy-Laurie Dickson, a technician working for Edison, and his team who is credited with doing most of the work on the development of the Kinetograph, which would later become the movie camera.

The modern business world requires teams of individuals to develop solutions to broad organizational problems. Take the simple example of developing a training program. An individual could conduct the required needs analysis, design and create all the necessary components, and track learning adoption across the organization. It is possible. But it is also a full-time job and potentially takes longer. It also pre-supposes that the individual has the requisite perspective, knowledge, and insight to do so. Worse, it deprives the organization of the ability to broadly learn from the creation of the program. It denies the insight and perspective of other parts of the organization that would make the program more effective. It doesn't leverage experts in the organization (such as data analysts) to ensure the final product is operationally sound, and thus requires reinvention of the wheel. And it doesn't create the secondary benefits of teaming that have the potential to influence the organization in positive ways.

I once worked with a L&D client group in a Fortune 500 company where this was exactly how they went about creating their learning programs. Each consultant developed learning programs for their clients depending on what gaps they were seeing. While the products were acceptable in terms of creating programs that sometimes influenced their client group, the fact that the consultants did them in relative isolation ensured that the products were less effective than they could be. This model failed to take into account broad gaps across all client groups, failed to generate learning content that could be accessed across the organization, and failed to holistically determine learning adoption. That is just the tip of the iceberg in terms of opportunities lost.

What if this L&D department created a cross-functional program team to tackle the problem of assessing needs, creating learning programs, and measuring adoption? Not only would they get the benefit of creating programs that were built upon a robust needs assessment, line input into content development, potential shared facilitation and delivery, and meaningful assessment of learning adoption; they would also have built relationships across the organization and generated a number of secondary teaming benefits. This may seem like a no brainer, but the model that this organization used is more common than you think.

In all manner of organizational work, teams are generally more effective than individuals in tackling broader organizational problems. Individuals have the ability to tackle a lot of work, but usually there are too many stakeholders, too many sub-specialties, and too many external and internal factors for any one individual to effectively manage. In most places we don't generally work on assembly lines anymore. And while that model has advantages in terms of scale and volume, it doesn't take into account the complexities of modern work.

The Teamwork Renaissance

In today's world, teaming and getting work done through teams is having a renaissance. Once upon a time almost nothing got done without a team. Then industrialization drove us to work in specialized roles on assembly lines and in workshops, and that tended to shape our worldview on how work got done. Eventually, large parts of the workforce traded assembly lines for cubicles, where managers tasked individuals to produce outputs that were handed off up the chain. There was little sense of the connectedness of the workplace. And of course, that is because it was largely disconnected. Old models of how work got done were shaped by the industrial revolution and its application of mass production methodologies, which culminated in the creation of those assembly lines and sweatshops. Indeed, mass production methodologies were introduced in all aspects of work and life.

Mass production and specialization drove, and were driven by, the changing goods and services technology introduced, and which were sorely needed by a growing US and world economy. One can easily see how difficult it would be for a single craftsman to build a locomotive alone. One could also imagine that building a locomotive would require a renaissance of teamwork, and in some ways it did, but its manufacture was largely completed by individuals specialized in very discreet tasks—in other words, a workgroup. A riveter may work all day riveting by himself, a welder the same; and never the two shall meet.

And now we are changing once again. Technology once atomized the workplace, and now it's bringing us back together. The modern world still leverages specialization but combines that specialization through a level of connectedness in ways once unimaginable. People the world over can now collaborate in real time, and cross-functional teams across the enterprise can quickly coordinate to ensure alignment, leverage the perspective of various disciplines, and manage stakeholders.

Technology also requires the collaboration of various disciplines. For example, healthcare organizations now need to collaborate with IT and data analytics to help them manage interconnected care systems and spot trends in patient outcomes. Even something as routine as creating a training program requires close cross-functional collaboration. Learning and development coordinates with IT functions, data analytics, marketing, and other departments to compile needs analysis, develop and deliver effective virtual and in-person training, and assess training effectiveness and skills adoption.

Once upon a time a few training professionals could develop and deliver such training, but with variable results across the enterprise. Now, technology requires and allows the teaming of various cross-functional stakeholders to develop and deliver training that is more likely to move the enterprise in the right direction. Organizations that can effectively leverage teaming and technology in these ways have a distinct competitive advantage.

In short, teaming is having a renaissance because technology is allowing, and indeed requiring, us to closely coordinate and collaborate to compete in the market. It doesn't matter what discipline you work in, organizations are recognizing that teams are now more necessary than ever to develop new systems and processes, create new products and services, embrace new ways of interacting with customers, and design new ways of doing business.

And with this teaming reemergence comes a need to revive our teamwork skills. We need to master how we collaborate effectively with others toward team goals. We need to build trust and safety with team members who recognize each person's unique contribution. We need to improve how we hold ourselves and others accountable.

Conclusion

When we fail to differentiate between teams and workgroups, we deny the organization the opportunity to develop the secondary benefits of teaming. We also erode trust. Teamwork matters. And as we shall see in the next chapter, effectively defining teams and purposefully thinking about how we will create and leverage them will generate a host of outcomes that engage your organization in ways that simply doing stuff cannot.

CHAPTER 2

Why Teamwork Matters

The short answer that most people will give as to why we team is so that we can get the stuff done that we can't do by ourselves. It is tough to build a house by yourself. It takes a long time and a lot of skill. But one of the most important aspects of teaming is that teams can provide you with solutions and innovations that you hadn't thought of before. Instead of thinking about the creation of teams as a way to get something done, it is a better idea to think of teams as a way to develop solutions. This is a powerful distinction and one that is often lost. If we think about it in this way, it influences how we build and manage our teams.

An example of this was an afternoon meeting I once had with Tim, an engineering leader whose department was having trouble developing its people. The lack of development meant that he couldn't assign people to different jobs because they had limited expertise across domains. It also meant that they couldn't rise through the organization to take on other positions. Tim was a quintessential engineering department leader—overworked and with way too much on his plate. It was hard to tell whether his rumpled sweater and tousled hair spoke to lack of interest in his appearance, or whether he just didn't have the time to care. He was a decent enough fellow though, and in the midst of too many change requests and too few engineers with too little time, he still wanted to figure out a way to develop his people. We talked for a while about how he might accomplish this.

Formal training was costly and there was already too little time. "How about simply using the work you already have as development?" I asked. "Think about who needs to do the work rather than who can do the work." He pondered this for a moment. "That's a good thought," he mused. "Maybe I'll get a few people together and have them come up with a formal succession plan and some kind of developmental rotation."

"That's good," I said, "but maybe you could build a team and let them know the problem you are trying to solve. And then let them figure out how to solve it? They may come up with something even better."

Tim nodded. "Sure, why not," he said with a wry grin. "I can barely figure out our budget at this point. Maybe they'll have some good ideas."

And so, Tim did just this. After some time, the team presented him with their engineering development program. It was an elaborate system whereby engineers could earn development points by engaging in any of a large selection of development activities. Each activity was weighted in terms of its development value. As engineers earned points, they climbed in readiness to move to other positions and roles. Each person was tracked in a spreadsheet so all could see the activities everyone was engaged in and the points they earned. A friendly competition of sorts developed, with engineers getting recognition for earning the most points in a quarter and year. You can imagine how the technical acumen of the department climbed and its bench strength grew as engineers engaged in a flurry of development.

The point of the story is that Tim had a problem and a solution in mind. He could have simply directed the team to create his solution. And he probably would have been relatively happy with that outcome. But by giving the team a problem and allowing them to develop the solution, they created something greater and more effective than anything that he would have come up with on his own. They created something he did not anticipate.

This story is instructive, and its lesson is fundamental to why we create teams. Optimally, we create teams to solve problems, not to simply do stuff. Those are different things. And, as we shall see, when we create teams to solve important problems, give them the autonomy to do so, effectively sponsor them, and provide them the resources to succeed, we are able to harvest ideas and benefits that we didn't anticipate. That is exactly why we create teams and why we should be purposeful about how we create them. Teaming, when done well, is a much bigger deal than simply giving a group a task. Teaming is creating the circumstances for innovation, ideas, and solutions heretofore unthought of. There is magic in this.

When we limit our teams to just doing stuff, we rob them of the innovative capacity that teams are capable of generating. We diminish the synergies of experience and perspective that teams can manifest as they seek out root causes and develop novel and value-added solutions to those problems. Individual leaders who task teams with something to do don't have all the answers, and it is arrogant to believe that they do. We must think of our teams as problem solvers, not activity-doers. Design teams with this in mind, and actually empower them to solve your most pressing problems.

In this chapter, we'll tackle four key reasons why teamwork and teams matter in the organization. Teams and teamwork solve broad organizational challenges. They create community, belonging, and purpose. They bring different perspectives to generate better ideas. And they advance shared organizational values and norms.

Building Teams to Solve Broad Organizational Challenges

In the modern workplace, getting important stuff done requires coordinated inputs across the entire organization. For example, once upon a time, HR departments could manage most of what they needed to do internally. Benefits management, recruiting, employee relations, and more were all done in-house and on paper. Modern HR organizations, on the other hand, need to closely partner with line organizations, IT, data analytics, legal, advertising, and marketing functions. Coordinating the inputs of all stakeholders is best accomplished through cross-functional teams to ensure the smooth development of products and services that meet the needs of all those stakeholders.

Teams have the ability to solve broad organizational challenges in ways that individuals simply cannot. As we've said, organizations are too large and complex, and the challenges they face are often too broad for individuals to tackle alone. Organizational change management efforts must take into account the many stakeholders and variables that influence not only the root cause of problems, but also the stakeholders and variables that we must contend with as we develop solutions to those problems. Cross-functional teams are necessary for tackling such complex problems.

Typically, the impetus for any change is a gap or failure that the organization is attempting to fill, mitigate, or improve upon. When departments attempt to develop solutions to larger organizational problems without getting sufficient input from line organizations, implementation is difficult, and failure is typical. Cross-functional teams are excellent vehicles for developing workable solutions that the organization will be likely to adopt. That is the important distinction here. Broad organizational adoption of change initiatives is often a function of whether recipients view the change as helpful. When the recipients of change do not see it as helpful, they will often reject it. This is not surprising. When stakeholders have input into the development of solutions and the ability to articulate what they can and cannot do, and what they are willing and unwilling to do, the end-state solution will likely have broader adoption across the organization.

An example of this is an HR organization I once worked with as they developed new performance management and talent development management processes for the organization. They identified what they considered gaps in those systems and attempted to develop enterprise solutions to those gaps. They wanted to add mentoring components, feedback mechanisms, check-in features, and development planning tools so that line leaders could more effectively develop their talent. This is all good stuff. In fact, I would characterize much of this as best practice . . . except that the line organizations didn't actually want much of it. Enormous sums of money, time, and effort were allocated to the development and implementation of a system that, in the end, was vastly underutilized. How did this happen?

The HR function didn't effectively leverage the line in the development of the solution. In fact, the line didn't even really know that there was a problem to be solved. In the words of one line executive, "This is a solution in search of a problem." How might this story have turned out differently? HR should have engaged in cross-functional teaming and allowed the team the autonomy to identify and solve the problem.

If HR had brought line executives and leaders into the problem statement development phase, they would have realized that development was happening organically across the organization, perceived gaps in talent pipelines were less meaningful than they actually were, and line leaders had far less time to engage with the tools than they realized. Had HR created a real cross-functional team with relevant stakeholders, allowed them to formulate the problem statement, and given them sufficient autonomy to create a viable solution, the end product would've been more accurate, and the solutions more readily adopted.

The most successful long-term and significant project outcomes I have seen occured when line organizations dedicated someone to be part of the team full-time. This is not always possible, given constraints in staffing and other factors, but it is optimal. Consulting with line organizations is good, but including full-time team members from the line is better. Line leaders are busy people and see consultations on such projects as just another thing to do. Their level of engagement is variable at best. When line leaders become actual team members, they develop a level of engagement with the project and process that mere consultation will not inspire. Line leaders who are part of the development of the products that affect them are also far more likely to use them and drive their implementation.

This dynamic has broader organizational implications. The purposeful use of cross-functional teams provides a platform for future coordination, communication, and collaboration. The relationships developed across departments, forged during the important work of a team, tend to persist. In the previous example of the performance management system, HR could have developed close relations with the line, IT, communications, and analytics that could be leveraged for future work. A level of trust could have developed between those on the team that might have translated to cross-functional communication and collaboration to proactively identify problems and strategically begin thinking about solutions. In other words, even after the team is disbanded, its members become cross-pollinators of ideas that can propel future innovations and team success.

The point of this story is that for all the benefits of teaming, much value can be lost when teams operate in organizational silos. It is critically important to ensure that the important work the team will be engaged in is actually important to the stakeholders who will be subject to the outputs of the team. Teaming, for all its other benefits, fundamentally exists to solve problems and thereby create value for the organization.

Consider This

- Design your team with representatives of the stakeholders who will be affected by the team's outputs. Partner with the people who will have to live with the solutions your team comes up with to identify the problem and develop the solution.
- Develop a strategic cross-functional perspective when thinking about the important work you intend for the team to engage in. Whatever problem you are trying to get the team to solve, and whatever change the team creates, will likely have impacts across the organization. Recognize this and influence line leaders to dedicate people to becoming actual team members.
- Ensure your teams are solving problems. If you are handing a team a problem and solution, that group is not solving a problem. Ensuring your teams are problem solving sets them up for success and allows the true benefits of teams to manifest themselves.
- Recognize that you probably don't have all the answers, and that a team of relevant stakeholders is best positioned to unearth root causes and create an effective problem statement. In this case, teaming starts well before the creation of the team. It starts with humility. And, as such, working to garner the diverse perspectives and needs of stakeholders is necessary for the team to be most successful.

Community, Belonging, and Purpose

The benefits of teaming go far beyond getting stuff done. When done well, teams can provide a high level of commitment and belonging, a clarity of duty that can generate a great deal of discretionary effort, and the circumstances for individual and organizational flourishing.

By and large, people enjoy working on teams—or, at least, well-functioning teams. People are social animals and the power of collective action provides a sense of shared success and belonging that really can't be overstated. We are wired for this. I remember as a young man, many years ago, attending a summer Outward Bound course. If you've never heard of Outward Bound, you should look into it—especially if you have kids.

Outward Bound is a wilderness course designed to help people understand that they are far more capable than they ever thought possible and to demonstrate the power of working together. My course was 30 days in the wilderness of upstate New York with a group of about 12 people and two instructors. We had to figure out how to survive together for a month in the mountains with limited supplies, braving the elements, climbing mountains, carrying canoes for miles, and shouldering 70 pound packs. The hard and important work was survival itself, and we could only succeed if we worked together. In the end, the sense of belonging and even victory was the most powerful I have ever experienced.

Through the suffering we shared to accomplish our goal, we came to love and believe in one another and ourselves in ways I didn't know were possible. I have never experienced anything quite like it. In fact, if I could design the ultimate leadership team building, it would look something like an Outward Bound program. Take an executive team and drop them off by helicopter 200 miles into the wilderness and tell them to find their way back home. I guarantee that if they survived, they would demonstrate all the characteristics of a great team: naked trust, real accountability, and unequivocal results. Through the shared suffering of engaging in the important work of survival, they would develop the teaming skills of accountability to the objective, and to one another. They would hone skills in challenge and compromise. They would, in the end, recognize that their differences were necessary to unravel and solve the challenges they shared.

In the modern world we rarely get to experience circumstances like that—circumstances our ancestors would readily recognize. And as wonderful as that is, it is also in some ways a shame. How many of us get to experience the power of being on a team like that? There are few circumstances that approach this, places where people have to mightily struggle together over long periods of time to succeed, such as competitive sports teams and the military.

It is through this lens that we can see why communities became one of the basic and powerful building blocks of human survival and progress. In the most basic sense, communities are simply teams of people working together to survive. In the ancient world, the natural formation of communities and their struggle to survive innately provided the elements required to create great teams. In our ability to survive without that struggle, we may have lost something important; something that has ironically necessitated the science of teamwork and books like this one. Something that humans once intuitively knew.

Indeed, it may be that the cadence of modern corporate life, or modern life for that matter, does not account for building the deep connections that only meaningful time shared through struggle can create. It does not necessarily provide for the mutual experiences that build shared understanding, empathy, and a temperance born of perspectives that we cannot see, except through the lens of people whose motivations we deeply know to be benevolent.

This is the power of teams. Teams mimic the power of community. This is the underlying framework that we feel when we are on a great team: the sense of belonging, purpose, fealty, duty, and love that drives levels of engagement that we do not see elsewhere. This is why teams are such powerful tools not only for accomplishing great things, but also for engaging people in our organizations in ways that simply sharing a space cannot.

Teams tap into and satisfy the ancient and eternal need for connection and belonging. Organizations that get this, and purposefully leverage it, drive levels of engagement not possible otherwise. It serves us well then to understand the power of belonging, shared purpose, values, and duty that a team can provide, and to work to emulate the conditions that generate such feelings. Imagine what could be accomplished in such circumstances. Imagine the power of your teams thus imbued.

Talent development is uniquely positioned to be the prime evangelist for this powerful benefit of teaming. In my experience, many leaders have little sense of what the power of community can provide to their organizations. They don't realize that this is what really drives organizational commitment and high levels of discretionary effort. Sure, teaming can get a lot of work done, but when done correctly, teaming generates communities that live long after the team is abandoned. This dynamic has the potential to build cross-functional connections and trust that enable problem identification, problem solving, and general organizational function. It creates relationships that catalyze coordination and collaboration.

If talent development can effectively help leaders to pause, think, and plan for these outcomes—outcomes that go far beyond whatever problem leaders are trying to solve—leaders have the opportunity to contribute to the creation of a high-performing organizational culture. A culture where people's sense of duty and loyalty to one another and to the organization generate high levels of discretionary effort and commitment. And isn't that what we are all looking to create? A culture where people are trying to figure out how to make the organization better? Where people consistently live up to their commitments and proactively solve problems? When people are part of a community, and engaged together in important work, that is what they do. Teaming is the most powerful tool we can leverage to create this sense of community.

> ### 🔆 **Consider This**
> - Community is developed through struggling together to accomplish important work. Without the struggle, there is no community and there is no team.
> - Great teams mimic the powerful and primal human connections of community. And it is this sense of community that generates loyalty, duty, and fealty to drive high levels of engagement, both to the team and to the larger organization.

Different Perspectives and Better Ideas

Teams get us to better solutions. People working in isolation come at problems with a singular perspective that inevitably leads to a singular solution. Group think aside, ideas are optimally vetted in the crucible of challenge, and the best solution manifests itself from that challenge. This is a critically important point and is largely the benefit of diversity and inclusion. We get better operational solutions when we have multiple perspectives and meaningful challenges. Teams, since they are composed of unique individuals with different ideas working on a difficult problem, provide a forum where differing perspectives can be vetted.

I was once on a team of organization development consultants who had a hard time planning, organizing, and making decisions. As a group, we loved to talk about ideas, but we had difficulty putting those ideas into action. In light of this, I thought we needed someone on the team with good organizational skills, more refined problem-solving skills, and a more utilitarian perspective to balance out our team. I recommended we hire someone with an engineering background to help us. They were aghast. "Can you imagine," they said, shaking their heads, "an engineer?!"

Sadly, they didn't bite on that recommendation and we continued to struggle. They did not recognize that problem solving is a critical teaming skill necessary to tackle difficult challenges. They failed to understand that teams should seek out different perspectives, challenge their groupthink, and recruit members with the necessary skills to tackle the problems they face.

Purposefully forming teams with different perspectives isn't too difficult as long as you remember to do it. However, in my experience, leaders often do not. Happily, this is a cultural attribute that can be developed. Talent development can help here. I have worked with several organizations that have purposefully created mechanisms that require them to build teams composed of people with varied backgrounds, disciplines, and personalities. For example, in a manufacturing organization I worked with we created a process requirement that, when creating teams, a proposed roster of the team would be submitted to the larger leadership team for review during weekly staff meetings. Leaders would weigh in on the team's composition to ensure that it had a healthy mix of people with not only the right technical skills, but also a blend of personalities and perspectives. This review usually took only minutes but provided a good backstop in ensuring the creation of a productive and dynamic team. A process like this ensures that leaders are actively thinking about this dynamic when creating teams rather than just hoping that they do. It forces leaders to stop and think about team makeup.

In this light, teaming is a connected set of skills that can be reinforced through the implementation of supportive processes. Put another way, it is one thing to recognize what one should do, and quite another to actually do it. Teaming is the creation of a process to ensure diverse perspectives. You can build accountability processes into your teaming efforts. Processes that drive accountability to best practices like the one outlined above go a long way to ensuring team performance.

This is not to say that creating diverse teams is always without significant challenge. Beware simply throwing different people together without the necessary skill to navigate differences and constructively challenge one another. Without such skill, you may inadvertently create a toxic brew that can hamper a team's progress. We will talk about managing team conflict in a later chapter, but suffice it to say that when done well, teams that combine differences tend to perform better than homogeneous teams. Craft your teams with this in mind to ensure you have lots of different approaches and ideas.

Creating Shared Organizational Values and Norms

Teams also create and enhance shared values and norms. Organizations with a coherent sense of their values and norms can find that teams strengthen and enhance them and even create new ones. Through working together day in and day out, under the correct leadership and with precise goals, good teams evolve ways of working together that work for them. The success of the team in growing and enhancing organizational norms and values also influences and enhances those larger organizational values. In other words, when organizational leaders pay attention, they will see evidence of what works in the smaller teams' success and begin to slowly adopt and emulate those behaviors and values.

Leadership that does not pay attention to this will lose out on these important lessons. Behaviors, values, and norms that work tend to have broader adoption over time than those that do not work. When teams demonstrate success in using particular practices, values, and norms, those team members can, and often do, proselytize them across the organization.

This evolutionary dynamic—the iterative process of trying different things and using the things that actually work—applies in the realm of cultural norms and values in the same way that it applies to the development of operational processes. Successful teams can significantly influence organizational culture over time through the broad dissemination of the shared team norms and values that brought them success. In this light, successful teams can be highly valuable in shaping and reshaping organizational culture.

For example, I helped the leaders in a department of a large regional healthcare provider craft a set of working norms that included the use of a designated challenger. The job of the designated challenger was to challenge team decisions in every meeting. No matter how obvious a decision was, the designated challenger thought of any and all ways that it was

---

👥 Consider This

- Seek out people who think differently. Diverse perspectives and experiences help teams generate better ideas and solutions. Without diverse perspectives and skills, teams will agree often but produce suboptimal solutions. They won't anticipate barriers and they likely won't create solutions that organizations will readily adopt.
- Creating processes to ensure teams follow through with their norms and best practices is necessary in all aspects of teaming. In this case, building a process to ensure diverse experiences and perspectives helps the organization purposefully create diverse teams.

---

a poor decision. Their job was, in essence, to find out what was wrong with the decision and to challenge the team to defend it. The role rotated among the members of the leadership team and after some reasonable practice they began to get good at it.

This simple change began to not only greatly influence the quality of their decisions, but also enhance their ability to challenge one another in constructive ways. Rather than people working up the courage to challenge the team and wondering whether they would be seen as a naysayer or not a team player, the rule was that they had to challenge it. Team members not only had permission to challenge, they were required to do so. This was a powerful norm, and it unleashed a level of creativity, decision-making quality, and constructive criticism skill-building that led the team to greater success than it had previously known.

Over time, as those team members moved across the organization to other departments, they brought that norm with them and began to implement it in their new roles. Thus, the broader culture began to move and change for the better, all because of this simple change that one team made. In effect, the team's efforts helped to evolve the organization.

The success of that new norm in helping to ensure better decision making, to inspire higher levels of engagement across the team, and to develop greater skill in constructive challenge was a clear demonstration to the organization that creating room for challenge was a norm that furthered the larger goals of the organization. In other words, challenge improved patient outcomes and patient satisfaction.

The vehicle for this change was the team. It was not an immediate and broad organizational change, which would probably not have worked. It was an incremental, evolutionary change started by a team, whose important goal was improving patient outcomes and patient satisfaction. The use of a team to essentially pilot a new norm is a powerful demonstration of its utility. Over time, the larger organization began to reward challenge rather than punish it. And a new organizational norm was introduced—a culture was incrementally changed.

The power of purposefully using teams to challenge groupthink and larger cultural issues cannot be overstated. Rather than using a Power-Point presentation or an article to move leaders to change their perspective, successful teams can tangibly demonstrate that thinking about and doing things in different ways can lead to outcomes that are beneficial to the metrics that leaders deeply care about.

 Consider This

- Teams can create new ways of doing things that can positively influence organizational culture. Organizations should be on the look-out for value-added systems and processes that teams create.
- Create processes and systems to drive team accountability, progress, and challenge. Instituting such processes keeps the team on track, keeps it focused, and smooths team function. When these processes work, they can be transmitted across the organization, thereby incrementally modifying the culture in useful ways. Work to build these systems and processes and evangelize those that work across the organization.

Conclusion

Teams are incredibly valuable. Certainly, they can get lots of work done, but that is just the beginning of it. When done well, they tend to more effectively diagnose root causes, develop more effective solutions, and solve our problems. Most importantly, they can generate a sense of trust and community that drives high levels of engagement. Over time, this dynamic pervades the organization. The sense of community that is created on teams struggling to accomplish important work lives on long after the team is disbanded. Those relationships remain. Team members continue to reach out to one another to share insights and to coordinate and collaborate. But teaming is not without its challenges. In the next chapter, we will explore some of those challenges and ways we might position ourselves to overcome them.

CHAPTER 3

Challenges to Teamwork

Teamwork has a number of challenges; otherwise we probably wouldn't have to write books such as this one. For example, there is a tension between getting diverse perspectives on our teams and, at the same time, honoring the cultures that serve our organization. Navigating this can be tricky. How we distribute work across the team is also an important consideration as we strive to ensure that the efforts of everyone on the team are necessary for success. Let's take a look at these challenges.

Distribution of Work

A critical attribute of team leadership and membership is the distribution of work. Team members can easily become discouraged when work is not distributed relatively evenly. When some team members are overloaded and others have little to do, it is common for problems to occur. We talked earlier about ensuring that team makeup is such that the skills and effort of every team member are required for the team to be successful. In addition to the inherent sense of value that comes with being needed on the team, team makeup influences how work is distributed.

In my work I have often seen organizations not pay much attention to how many people are on the team or the mix of skills they bring to the team. Having too many people on the team contributes to uneven distributions of work—some team members often have lots to do, while others have too little. Having too many people also fosters a sense of "I don't really have to do this because someone else will certainly take care of it."

This breeds lack of ownership. Team leaders must therefore take care that they have the correct number of people on the team as well as the correct mix of skills and talent. This goes a long way toward ensuring that everyone feels important and like they are being fairly treated.

An important consideration for team leaders and team members is the Pareto Principle. The Pareto Principle can be applied to many things, but for the purposes of work distribution, it states that 20 percent of the people do 80 percent of the work. I am sure that every reader has seen this in action, and perhaps it is an obvious point. What we learn from the Pareto Principle, however, is that you must be vigilant in monitoring who does the work and how much of it they do.

Certainly, the work of teams rises and falls in any given unit of time. Sometimes people with a particular skill set are working a great deal before they hand off work to another subset of people with a different skill set. One can easily imagine program designers working very hard before they hand their work over to editors who will go over it with a fine-toothed comb. These two groups will offer considerable energy toward the goal of providing a high-quality development program, but at different times. It is therefore important that leaders and team members broadcast the aggregate inputs of team members so that everyone understands that everyone else has significantly contributed to the work.

If some team members begin to accumulate too much of the work contribution, you need to figure out why. It may be that the team needs to direct other team members to help with that portion of the work, some team members have too little to do, or you have too few people with a certain skill set. Whatever the reason, incorrect work distribution is a major contributor to team disengagement and low morale. Either the overworked individuals become resentful, or other team members begin to feel less valuable, or both.

It can be tempting as a team leader to essentially ignore this dynamic. After all, the work is getting done and your high-performing individuals are taking care of business. You might have too much on your plate, and engaging with this problem might seem like a less-than-useful occupation of your time. Team members can easily fall into this trap as well. After all, if someone else is doing the work, then you are not. Beware of this kind of thinking. In the short-term this may not feel like a problem, but the long-term implications to team morale can be extremely negative. Once team members begin to feel that they are taking on an inordinate amount of work, they will likely begin to feel resentment and disengage.

You can use the purposeful challenge culture and curiosity culture discussed in later chapters to talk about work distribution. There should be nothing negative about bringing up workload and disparities in work distribution. It is such an important dynamic to team functioning that teams should make it a point to talk about work distribution during team huddles and team meetings.

An L&D group I once worked with did exactly that, to good effect. Regularly asking questions such as, "How is your workload? What negatives are you experiencing related to your workload? What positives are you experiencing related to your workload?" gave participants license to express themselves. Leaders, through frequent one-on-ones, should probe their teams and have a good idea of how much work team members are doing, so they can distribute and redistribute work accordingly. This may seem like an obvious point, but it's one of those basic leadership behaviors that often gets lost. Make it a point to probe workload when having one-on-ones with team members with an eye not only for identifying instances of too much work, but also too little.

Creating a process to ensure focus on work distribution is a good idea. As I keep reiterating, without a process, you are unlikely to maintain focus over time. The work and pace of the work is often such that three months have gone by before you realize you haven't checked on work distribution. Make it a practice to insert a discussion about work distribution into monthly project status meetings. If it's a recurring item on your agenda you won't lose sight of it.

Consider This

- Purposefully distribute work so that each member is carrying their fair share of the load. And maintain a close connection with team members so you have a clear understanding of how much work each member is doing. Keep a watchful eye on the Pareto Principle and redistribute work as needed.
- Develop team norms that encourage and allow the team to talk meaningfully about work distribution. One of the building blocks of great team development is in the shared work that the team must shoulder.
- Create processes to ensure that team leaders are monitoring work distribution through one-on-ones, frequent group huddles, and even publicly viewable progress tools. Team members need to feel comfortable verbalizing their workload and asking for help. This not only short-circuits the Pareto Principle, but it also allows team members to pitch in. This dynamic is powerful in creating the circumstances where great teams form. In a real way, shared work, or shared suffering, is a prerequisite to the formation of great teams. As such, it is imperative that leaders and team members ensure the work is truly shared.

Diverse Teams and Roadblocks to Constructing Them

Leaders have to go with the horses they have in the stable, as the saying goes. If the talent pool available to a leader is composed of mostly the same kind of people, there may not be people around who can fill the different roles that create conditions for great teams. All fields and disciplines tend to struggle with this dynamic.

For example, highly technical fields are often filled with engineers, scientists, or mathematicians whose personality, training, and disposition are well suited for excellence in their chosen field, but they are also not commonly very diverse. HR functions are similarly populated with people whose worldview and training are similar. This makes sense. Those who have little enthusiasm for interacting with other people don't tend to make very good HR people. And so, even when leaders think to populate a team with diverse perspectives, sometimes they simply don't have a good selection of people to choose from. This is also confounded by the fact that everyone is probably working on various projects already, and leaders can't pick everyone they want to be on a team.

Organizations that do have people of differing backgrounds and perspectives that can help in the formation of excellent teams often have only a limited quantity of those people. An outgoing, creative, out-of-the-box thinking engineer may be relatively rare. What often happens in organizations who purposefully try to populate teams with diverse inputs is that the few different people in the organization are almost always chosen to be on teams.

If the directive is to populate teams with diverse perspectives, then leaders will seek them out. I once worked with an engineer in a technical organization who was exhausted from being on so many teams and workgroups. Every time the organization needed someone who was creative and innovative, she was selected.

The short answer to all of this is that there is no short answer. Focusing on the root cause of the problem, we need to work with recruiting and hiring managers to ensure that the organization hires lots of different kinds of people. Leaders must then manage the technical requirements of positions versus other attributes they want people to bring to the table.

Weighing technical or regulatory job requirements versus other criteria for their organization is a lot for leaders to think about. Managing all these priorities may be difficult, but recognizing the potential problem is critical in successfully navigating, or at least improving, the quality and quantity of diverse voices in the organization.

In the absence of diverse talent in your organization, it makes sense to develop strategies to think differently. The Color Team is a useful process to drive people to think differently. As the team works through the various phases of the project, you can purposefully create short-term subgroups whose job it is to literally think differently.

For example, at each phase of project development, create:

- A Red Team whose job is to find fault and anticipate problems
- A Purple Team to innovate solutions
- A Green Team to brainstorm potential positive impacts the solution might have across the organization

The point here is to create a system for the kind of thinking you want at any given time so that those not wired that way can attempt to engage in diverse thinking. This does not have to be an elaborate endeavor. Groups can engage in this at any time. Their utility is to simply provide a framework that drives diverse thinking.

A good example of this is an HR group I worked with, which was populated with very energetic young people who had similar backgrounds and styles. While they got along great and were eager to tackle whatever challenge was placed in front of them, they were not very good at thinking through what could go wrong. They were not wired for challenging each other or the trajectory of the project. The end result was that they often identified what they thought was a potential problem and eagerly rushed into solution development. Questioning the trajectory of the project or its assumptions was not in their DNA. In fact, it was frowned upon. This resulted in projects and programs that often failed to solve problems and fell short of project objectives. As with many groups suffering from groupthink, there were too many unthought-of barriers and root causes that the team failed to anticipate. No one on the team was wired to challenge, question, and generally think about why the team was wrong in its approach.

The solution was to create a process whereby the group would put on their Red Team hats at the beginning of the project and brainstorm what was wrong with their assumptions, what was wrong with their plan, and what could go wrong in its implementation. This certainly put them outside their comfort zone. But by getting them in a room and challenging them to think negatively, they were given license to do just that. At first, they weren't very good at it, but by incorporating this activity into the start of their projects, they got better. They began to uncover unanticipated roadblocks, barriers, and pitfalls that they were then able to proactively account for in the development of their plans.

Implementing this process into how they went about scoping projects forced them to think differently. It would be better if they had folks on the team who could naturally challenge them in this way. If so, perhaps this process wouldn't have been necessary. But even in the absence of this kind of diverse thinking, implementing this process forced them to think a new way. And that made all the difference.

 Consider This
- As you build diverse teams, be mindful of not overusing your diverse talent. They tend to be vectored to every team you have. This is sometimes unavoidable.
- If you find that you cannot create a team composed of people who think differently, create a process to drive divergent thinking. The Color Team process is a useful way to push people out of their comfort zone and encourage divergent thinking.
- Make it safe to share divergent thinking, and encourage it.

Leader and Organizational Bias

Leaders and teams are subject to the same biases that we all fall prey to. They naturally tend toward people like themselves; people with similar backgrounds, perspectives, worldviews, and values. This is pretty normal stuff.

The concept of organizational fit is a pathology that can hinder team effectiveness—and, indeed, organizational effectiveness more broadly—by limiting the kinds of people an organization hires, develops, promotes, and puts on teams. However, there is also a utilitarian perspective to these workplace biases that is worth considering, and which I see very often. This is something TD professionals need to be aware of when thinking about organizational and team makeup.

A lot has been written about organizational culture and, in my mind, it is often overcomplicated. Simply put, organizational culture is the output of what the organization rewards and punishes as it attempts to achieve its goals by whatever metric it finds meaningful. This is pretty obvious when you think about it. Healthcare organizations value success in not only patient outcomes, but also patient satisfaction. Their organizational culture is highly influenced by these metrics. They care about getting patients better and how patients experience their care. Healthcare organizations use extensive metrics and key performance indicators (KPI) to track these outcomes. People who effectively navigate these KPIs are rewarded, while people who do not are punished. The organization thus evolves behaviors that are most efficacious in making that outcome happen. If you are an ego-centric and nasty person, you probably won't be too successful in healthcare by these standards (unless you are a surgeon). Further, people who are naturally disposed to think and act in certain ways tend to gravitate toward professions that support those aims and values. The evolutionary development of this culture tends to reinforce these attributes in a virtuous cycle that year-over-year tends to improve both patient outcomes and patient satisfaction. This is a good thing for healthcare organizations and their patients.

This happens in all professions. To take another example, production organizations value precision and action orientation. They often have little time for feelings and "woo-woo." And in their mind, rightly so. They have not seen those kinds of behaviors and beliefs benefit their quest to manage their own KPIs, which are usually centered around on-time and under-budget measurements.

In all organizations, leaders naturally tend to value people with personalities, interests, and characteristics that match the dominant cultural attributes of the organization, which in turn match the attributes most typically associated with excellence in whatever line of work we are talking about. And while our first reaction is to flinch at this obvious bias toward one viewpoint, it is actually an extremely useful dynamic. It isn't any more useful to have someone who doesn't pay attention to technical details occupy a difficult technical position than it is to have a a taciturn person who dislikes people occupy a customer service role. Tending to hire, develop, and promote people who have attributes valuable to achieving our organizational goals isn't weird. However, it isn't necessarily a good thing when it comes to gathering different perspectives that can effectively challenge the organization and its teams.

Further exacerbating all of this is the fact that regardless of KPIs and the characteristics that drive KPI fulfilment, people generally like to hang out with people like themselves. While this is a natural phenomenon, it isn't very useful to the health of the organization. One can make a pretty good argument that hiring for culture fit to ensure we can fulfill our KPIs and success measurements is a good thing. It is tougher to make the argument that hiring people just because we happen to think they are cool is good for the organization. From an organizational success perspective, the downsides of cultural homogeneity far outweigh the upsides of having your drinking buddy work with you.

The obvious potential negative outcome of this is the development of groupthink. The organization is filled with people who are fundamentally the same—they think the same, value the same things, have similar backgrounds and educations, and often similar personalities. This leads to the same solutions, the same approaches, and the same answers every time. But again, this dynamic does serve a useful purpose—that is why it exists. However, when market conditions change, how does the organization respond? Are employees nimble, innovative, and able to pivot to meet new customer demands? Does the team have the necessary agility to change directions and innovate unique ways of thinking about things to provide the greatest value?

For example, the nuclear industry is, in many ways, an industry designed to work in a regulated market in the 1960s and 1970s. The nuclear regulatory environment is overwhelming and costly. After the Three Mile Island incident in 1979, the industry went through enormous regulatory changes to ensure that nothing like that ever happened again. Regulators demanded levels of oversight, both internally and externally, that required huge numbers of people to constantly monitor systems, processes, inputs, and outputs. As a result, operating costs went sky high. This was doable in the 1980s, when operators could relatively easily pass costs on to consumers. Then, in the 1990s, markets began to deregulate. Operating costs could no longer be passed onto consumers and the nuclear industry struggled to adapt.

However, even as operating margins decreased, nuclear energy was still a viable industry. Energy costs were relatively high and the industry found that it could still make a decent profit despite the regulatory burden. The third blow to the industry occurred with the advent of fracking. Natural gas prices plummeted, and energy costs began a downward trend. As a result, the costs the nuclear industry incurred through their operating model began to become unsustainable. The operating model the nuclear industry adopted to compete in energy markets and ward off regulators essentially revolved around perfect operational execution, every day, every time, in everything. Perfection became the goal, the mantra, and the orthodoxy. The problem is, perfection is incredibly costly.

For example, safety is of primary concern in the nuclear industry—one could argue, as it should be in any industry. People getting hurt on the job is unacceptable if we can prevent it. However, perfect safety, meaning no one gets hurt, ever, is a costly goal. The law of diminishing returns applies, and the cost curve begins to exponentially rise the closer you get to perfection. With this in mind, and applied to all aspects of its operations, it is easy to see how the nuclear industry is becoming financially unviable. And it is also easy to see how its leaders, who are adherents to the religion of perfection, are having an increasingly difficult time adjusting their business model to changing market dynamics.

How do you go from an orthodoxy of perfection to believing in good enough? The groupthink that provided the nuclear industry with great success in markets where money was abundant and cost consideration were negligible has proven to be less useful in markets where cost considerations have to become much more prominent.

To be fair, the nuclear industry is in a tough spot. Public perceptions are such that a posture that suggests anything less than perfection would not be viewed positively. However, there are plenty of places where good enough is OK, but there are few voices in the industry that can effectively advocate for that change. Leadership is derived from those whose mental model is grounded in the quest for perfection and to whom good enough seems almost an apostasy. If you are going to do something, do it perfectly well, as they say. You can take that literally, or you can take it figuratively. Doing it perfectly well, in many cases, is good enough.

Talent and organization development (OD) cultures are no different. They too attract people with similar backgrounds, similar educations, and similar experiences. They read the same books and articles and their worldview is often virtually identical. They agree with each other often and easily. But the downsides to groupthink in OD culture are similarly negative. Remember the reaction to my suggestion that we hire an engineer into our OD group in chapter 2?

While the dynamic of hiring for cultural fit is natural, and often even useful, it clearly has its drawbacks. Cultural attributes develop for a very good reason and are demonstrably useful, and yet they lead to groupthink, loss of innovative capacity, and a less nimble and adaptive organization. It is critically important for leaders and talent professionals to be aware of, and wary of, this dynamic. Pointing out groupthink behaviors, and specifically highlighting the negative outcomes they cause, can help leaders begin to take action to integrate other voices, perspectives, and ways of thinking into the organization. Purposefully using teams to demonstrate the utility of leveraging these different voices is a powerful tool for shifting the cultural framework that organizations can become trapped in.

Consider This

- Groupthink is a thing for a reason. It often works. Teams need to recognize the value of organizational bias in that it can help the organization achieve its objectives. However, there is a distinct downside to groupthink that inhibits innovation and organizational agility.
- Insist, to the extent possible, that your teams be populated with people who do not conform to organizational biases. Build processes that provide checkpoints when a team is created to assess its makeup and populate it with a diversity of thought.

Conclusion

How we populate our teams with diverse perspectives while ensuring that they represent the cultural attributes that make our organization successful is important. How we distribute work across the team to ensure the efforts and energies of everyone on the team are engaged for success is critical. It is vital that leaders and talent development purposefully think about these factors as they build and deploy teams. This is part of setting our teams up for success. Crafting teams in the TD space is no different, but there are some relatively unique considerations that tend to derail TD teams. Since TD organizations do not usually have much power to direct line organizations, how they build their teams and set them up for success is sometimes a bit different.

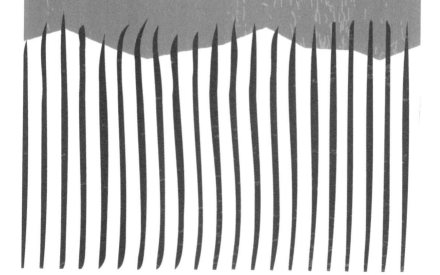

PART 2

Teamwork and Talent Development

CHAPTER 4

Why Teamwork Matters in Talent Development

In talent development organizations, teaming and teamwork have become more important than ever. The interconnectedness of the organization now requires talent development to forge relationships to be most effective. Gone are the days when solo practitioners sat in lonely cubicles developing content and processes only to reveal them to little fanfare and weak uptake.

In my experience, the most common reason for failure in most areas of talent and organization development is a lack of executive sponsorship and a lack of coordination and collaboration with line and support organizations in the development of change and talent initiatives. There are a couple of reasons for this.

Using Teams to Ensure Buy-In

The primary reason is that most TD and OD initiatives are not organically important to most executive and line leaders. For the most part, line leaders are entirely too busy with operational concerns to be motivated to implement the latest TD process or change initiative. This is especially true for initiatives that address broad cultural norms and behaviors, which often take a good deal of time to bear fruit and require significant behavior changes from line leaders. When faced with this reality, line leaders are often too jaded to meaningfully engage with whatever behavior change TD is advocating.

For example, in working with an organization on improving pipelining and talent development, the TD group developed a career mapping initiative that required leaders to engage in frequent one-on-ones, fill out career mapping plans, enter them into the system, and meet with all employees regularly to monitor progress toward readiness. This seemed like a great idea, and the TD organization unveiled it to great fanfare. The problem was that the line had no input into its development, and had little interest in implementing it. They were already too busy and saw little immediate value in engaging with the processes.

In other words, the development of talent is a long-view activity. The benefits of that endeavor would not manifest for some time. It might take years of dutifully implementing the process to see significant improvement in the talent pipeline and developmental readiness for senior roles. And while we would hope that leaders intrinsically see the value in such talent development activities, for the most part they do not. And, they are not typically rewarded for those behaviors.

To make matters worse, the fact that the TD group did not typically coordinate and cooperate with the line when developing their initiatives in years prior ensured that they had not been very successful in implementing those programs. It is this dynamic that leads to the perspective of the line that whatever new thing TD produces is just another flavor of the day. Operational leaders will roll their eyes with the full expectation that this new initiative would be gone and replaced with yet another within a year or two. It cannot be overstated how much time and resources are wasted in developing solutions that are destined to fail because the people who actually have to execute them are not involved in their development.

Had TD partnered, collaborated, and coordinated with the line in determining a root-cause problem statement, and developed initiatives to address those root causes with actions that line leaders had a hand in designing and, most importantly, were willing to commit to, such programs would have a much better chance of being adopted by the organization.

When I say that TD organizations should team with line organizations in the development of TD initiatives, I can already hear you thinking, "Well of course, I already do that." And yet, everywhere I go, I see failures that are directly related to a lack of coordination and collaboration with line leaders. It is not enough to talk to a line leader or two in the planning stage, get their tacit agreement, and believe they were a part of the development team. That does not constitute collaboration. Line leaders need to actually be a part of the team from the development of the problem statement, to the creation of solutions, to their deployment, and beyond. And if the line cannot offer someone to be a part of the team, then by definition the initiative is not important enough to them, and should be reevaluated.

People and organizations will find the resources and time to prioritize what is important to them. It is the same dynamic that occurs when I say that I do not have time to exercise. The fact is, I could make time to exercise if it was important enough to me. I will offer that the first step in developing TD initiatives is for TD leaders to effectively contract with senior leaders to direct effective resources to the problem statement. If you cannot convince senior leaders to allocate appropriate resources, then perhaps the problem statement is not compelling enough, or your senior leaders do not see it as a problem worth solving. The importance of TD teaming with the line is critical to effectively engage the organization.

An objection that I often hear from TD professionals is that senior leaders don't understand the importance of their initiatives, and so will not allocate resources to improve the chance that the initiative will be successful. For example, many senior leaders do not think that meaningfully supporting TD initiatives is worth the time and money. TD professionals will assert that in order for executives to understand the value of their initiatives, executives need to see them in action, whether they actually want them or not. In other words, the thinking is that if we build and implement it, executives will see how great and valuable it is, which will then drive accountability. The problem with that is, without executive sponsorship and resource allocation, the initiative probably won't be successful. Executives then slowly nod and think, "Yeah, I was right. That isn't a thing worth investing in." And so they will be less likely to invest in future initiatives.

The remedy for this is for TD organizations to leverage the power of teams. TD needs to model how teams most effectively form and function, and then use that model to collaborate with line leaders to pilot small-scale versions of their initiatives. Once value is shown, they can prompt effective executive sponsorship and funding. It cannot be overstated how important this dynamic is when undertaking whatever change initiatives you are contemplating, even more so in the TD space.

Time and again I see the development and rollout of large-scale changes that do not have sufficient sponsorship to succeed. This lack of sponsorship goes a long way to assure failure. Repeated failure or subpar returns on the expected value of the project demoralizes current and future teams. While this is not a book about change management, this dynamic directly influences the behavior and success of current and future teams—success breeds success and failure breeds failure.

If you are positioning the team to fail, then it doesn't much matter how great you are at leading teams or being a team member. The most important initial action of teaming then is to position the team for success by gaining sufficient executive sponsorship, either up front or by piloting small-scale initiatives to show value. Then build a team with sufficient line membership so that the end users will have been co-creators of that output, thereby increasing the chances that they will adopt the change. This is setting the team up for success.

Consider This

- Contract with leaders to ensure that whatever your team is trying to do is valued by the people who will be impacted by it. And that it is not a solution in search of a problem. Without effective contracting, the output of your teams can easily fail and become just another flavor of the day.

- Recognize the power of small-scale pilots to demonstrate value. Too often teams are created to solve a problem that leaders in the organization do not understand or see. These solutions often mean more work for them as well. While TD may see real value, if the line doesn't similarly see the value, they will under-resource it, and then conclude it was not a great idea. Small-scale pilots executed by well-formed, well-led teams, with sufficient autonomy to create value-added solutions, can demonstrate real value to leaders in the organization—which will often be enough to get the sponsorship you need to proceed.

- It's OK if the pilot reveals that it wasn't such a great idea. Teams shouldn't be wedded to an outcome that the data doesn't support. Team leaders and team members can, and should, continuously monitor progress and results so that the output is valuable and workable.

Teamwork and Talent Development Capabilities

We've covered how teamwork and teaming beyond just the talent development function can help ensure buy-in and executive support. But teamwork matters in nearly every behavior and skill a talent development professional needs to have or be able to do. In this sense, we can look to the Talent Development Capability Model.

Under the Building Personal Capability domain, teamwork skills naturally influence one's ability for leadership and collaboration. This extends to facilitating collaboration, fostering environments that encourage respectful relationships, communicating effectively, providing feedback, and assessing the work of others. Teamwork is also important for managing projects, such as being able to plan, organize, direct, and control resources for a finite period to complete specific goals and objectives. As we've stated before, teamwork skills tie into your awareness of diversity and inclusion within the team's makeup.

Figure 4-1. Talent Development Capability Model

Building Personal Capability	Developing Professional Capability	Impacting Organizational Capability
• Communication • Emotional Intelligence & Decision Making • Collaboration & Leadership • Cultural Awareness & Inclusion • Project Management • Compliance & Ethical Behavior • Lifelong Learning	• Learning Sciences • Instructional Design • Training Delivery & Facilitation • Technology Application • Knowledge Management • Career & Leadership Development • Coaching • Evaluating Impact	• Business Insight • Consulting & Business Partnering • Organization Development & Culture • Talent Strategy & Management • Performance Improvement • Change Management • Data & Analytics • Future Readiness

With the Developing Professional Capability domain, teamwork skills influence how you create the processes, systems, and frameworks that foster learning, maximize individual performance, and develop the capacity and potential of employees. Even solo talent development professionals need to work with others from the organization in teams to design and deliver training, career, and leadership development programs.

For the Impacting Organizational Capability domain, when talent development professionals improve their teamwork skills, they better ensure their ability to drive organizational performance, productivity, and operational results. Teamwork skills affect your ability to serve as a performance consultant and business partner to the functions you support, as well as to facilitate and enable change.

Conclusion

We've talked about the importance of teams to the organization. Teams are not only positioned to get work done, they are also powerful vehicles to solve problems and promote positive culture change by introducing new behaviors and cultural norms. The best senior leaders cultivate norms that position teams to create and address root-cause problem statements. And good teams distill decision making through challenge and inquiry to develop solutions. Successful teams, engaged in important work, imbue their members with a sense of belonging and purpose that captures high levels of engagement and discretionary effort to identify problems and design and deploy innovative solutions. Well-formed teams also promote a diverse and inclusive culture in which different perspectives, experiences, and backgrounds are valued and sought out. In essence, the development of a teaming culture is one of the most powerful differentiators you can deploy to propel your organization to higher levels of engagement and profitability.

Given the importance of teams to the organization, it behooves us to think about how we can most effectively lead teams and position ourselves to contribute to the teams we are on. We may be wired for teamwork, but that's not to say that we are necessarily good at it. Like anything, effective teaming is a skill that can be learned. While we may intrinsically build relationships and naturally wish to come together with others in many ways, there are a number of soft skills that great team leaders and team members must develop to ensure a team's effectiveness.

In my work, I am often called to help teams be more effective. In the many years I have been working with teams, I have developed a checklist of what I look for in a team. When they do these things well, they are far more likely to be effective. Team development, rather than being a set of disconnected skills and attributes, is an iterative process whereby the adoption of certain behaviors and actions facilitates the development of complementary behaviors and actions that lead to the desired outcome. These behaviors build upon one another and lead to a virtuous cycle of development that culminates in an effective team. Without each of the behaviors in place, teams are less likely to generate progress towards the next one.

In other words, while we can develop individual teaming skills such as ensuring the selection of diverse teams and being open to different perspectives, the process of teaming, when done well, is what makes those individual skills useful. In the absence of effective teaming circumstances, those individual skills are less useful. We have all been on teams where we try to be open to different perspectives, but the teaming culture is such that different perspectives are not valued. If the teaming culture is not correctly formulated, then our teaming skills will not have positive impact. And we will likely get frustrated and disengaged.

The model of how this fits together looks like Figure 4-2. Without important and clear goals, people will have less interest in generating the kind of genuine curiosity that facilitates effective challenges to the status quo. After all, if the work isn't important, then what is there to be curious about? If we approach our work and team with a genuine sense of curiosity, we are given greater license to challenge one another, ask questions, and disagree. And as we shall see, constructive disagreement and struggle leads to different ideas, perspectives, and better solutions. Progress can then be most effectively made.

Figure 4-2. Team Effectiveness Progression

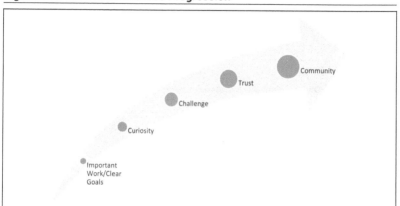

In the struggle of working together, striving to accomplish an important task, wrestling with ideas, and working through differences, trust emerges. As we begin to see that we can rely on one another, that we are trustworthy, that we care about our important work and each other, we begin to trust one another. And that is when the kind of community and belonging that great teams exhibit emerges. Teams then begin to generate loyalty not only to the important work, but also to each other. This is the model. While other models outline the characteristics of teams, they often do not outline the behaviors that build great teams.

In the upcoming chapters, I will walk you through this framework to help you use the power of teaming to drive organizational engagement and success.

CHAPTER 5
Frame the Work

Are you building a wall or a cathedral? When doing the work, it is easy to think we are just building a wall. After all, in some sense, a cathedral is just a collection of walls. But that is not very inspiring. A wall may be important, but its framing doesn't make one believe they are involved in something truly worthy of their best efforts. But when we are building a cathedral, the perspective becomes completely different. In that case, we are engaged in the creation of something magnificent. We are part of something amazing that has the great potential to change the world.

Consider that York Minster Cathedral took 252 years to build. For perspective, that is longer than the United States has been in existence. Construction started in 1220 and was completed in 1472. It took generations of stone masons, carpenters, and project managers laboring for centuries to complete what has been called the greatest cathedral north of the Alps. How important was the work to those people that they would dedicate their entire lives to creating such a structure? Surely, they would not do so if they were merely constructing a wall, even though that was in essence exactly what they were doing. To them, the larger work was important enough to dedicate their entire lives to.

Now, the work we do may not rise to that level of importance. But framing the value of our work using that question—"Are we building a wall or a cathedral?"—is an instructive exercise that can help us figure out why we are doing what we are doing.

Why Framing Matters
We've touched on this before, but it bears repeating. Important work is the primary driver of team effectiveness. Effective teams require dedication,

effort, and commitment from every team member. If the work you are engaged in is not important, then it is unlikely that people will generate the kind of effort required to do the best work that the team can do.

Too often, leaders don't think much about this. They pull a team together and get them going without much thought about the framing. But important work is foundational to the construction of highly effective teams. It creates conditions whereby people will be willing to not only work hard but also engage in the uncomfortable work of building trust, being vulnerable, challenging one another, and being curious about an opinion or perspective that is at odds with their own. Important work helps people lay down their egos and sublimate themselves to the collective effort. Important work is the enabler of all the functional behaviors of effective teams. Without it, those functional behaviors likely won't happen, and we won't have a team. Therefore, how we frame the work to our teams is a leadership and team skill that is fundamental to team success.

Important work is just that—it is work that is meaningfully attempting to fix something or build or innovate a new product or service that provides greater value for the organization. It is work that meaningfully makes a difference. This is a critical point. By this definition, a decent amount of work in the organization isn't all that important. Lots of work is administrative or maintenance-oriented—duties that keep the machine running and the gears of the organization turning. It is important in that it allows the organization to continue functioning, but it isn't very important in terms of what inspires people or teams.

More corrosive is the work built around what I call brand management. This is work that is designed to market the department or function to the larger organization and to demonstrate its importance or value. It is typical in HR and support organizations that do not have a direct impact on the core functions of the company that actually make the money and have trouble quantitatively measuring value.

For example, it is difficult to quantify the ROI of a leadership development program. In the absence of measurable value, support organizations often develop proxies for value, such as quantity of stuff produced. In other words, we may not be able to quantitatively demonstrate value, but we can sure create a lot of stuff! I have seen a good deal of brand management over the years as support executives direct resources to showcase the supposed value that their department can bring to the organization. This dynamic is largely fueled by the idea that we need to be doing something, virtually anything, rather than doing nothing. And so, support executives create solutions to minor problems and offer them up to the larger organization as a demonstration of value.

Broadly speaking, this is a dangerous practice, especially as it relates to teams and teaming. What I have noticed is that people generally understand when they are engaged in unimportant work. They sense that the rhetoric of executives and leaders selling them on the importance of unimportant work is disingenuous.

This dynamic not only limits the benefit of teaming, but it degrades trust and breeds antipathy that will, over time, seep into the psyche of future teams in the organization. When exposed to such busywork, people will begin to question the veracity of future teams and future work. I would strongly encourage readers to be honest about the work they do and the work they assign to teams in the organization. It is far better to be honest about the work and be honest about the motives of the work.

Important Work as a Litmus Test

In this sense, attempting to frame the importance of your work can become somewhat of a litmus test as to whether you should actually be doing that work at all. If you can't find a way to connect the work in some important way to advancing the department, organization, community, or world, then it may not be worth doing. This is important. The cost of unimportant work is high, not only in time and resources wasted, but, as we've seen, in the negative effect it has on anyone who touches it.

One helpful strategy is to articulate the reason you are doing the work and see if it sounds ridiculous. If it does, then it probably is. For example, if I were to say, "The reason we are doing this work is so that the organization will think we are useful," one might think that isn't such a great reason to dedicate lots of time and energy to a project.

Or imagine if a leader were to say, "The creation of this webinar will greatly increase the competence and capacity of our leaders to lead." If someone believes that a webinar does not have the power to do that, they might conclude that the work isn't all that important. The webinar may be somewhat valuable, but probably not in the way we just articulated it. Another way to put it might be to say, "The webinar will incrementally add value to our learning portfolio." That is probably true, is more honest, and may be something that people can get behind.

You could instead frame the work that the webinar is a component of a larger and important development strategy. Don't oversell. The webinar itself may not be that important in the grand scheme of things, but the incremental contribution of the webinar to drive the development strategy can make it important.

This is an example of how to frame work that might *seem* unimportant, but *is* important in reality. This is a critical teaming and team leadership skill. When work seems unimportant, it may be that it is a component of some larger, important work. Seek out links to the larger important work so you can properly frame it to the team. You can even use the team to seek out the importance of the work. Doing so can prompt a meaningful conversation that has the potential to generate a clear understanding around the relative importance of the work.

In framing important work, one might ask a couple of questions to probe its importance. It doesn't necessarily have to tick every one of these boxes, but it will definitionally tick at least some. Ask:

- How will effectively implementing the work impact the larger organization?
- What benefits will the organization realize?
- How does the work meaningfully help us achieve our goals and vision?

- How does the work connect to the individual and their development and future prospects in the organization?
- How does the work connect with something a prospective team member is currently interested in?

Framing Work to Drive Interest

Framing the importance of the work is a critical skill component in teaming and team creation. As we've said, if the work is not important, then you probably don't have a team. But framing the importance of the work is also critical in generating enthusiasm and engagement. After all, the work may be important, but unless the team sees it that way, then it becomes functionally unimportant. This is a critical distinction. You can, and should, appeal to prospective team members in a variety of ways to communicate the importance of the work.

Once you've determined that the work is actually important, you can foster interest that connects to the work. Even if the work isn't initially very compelling to an individual, you can appeal to the fact that it might be something an employee needs to get better at doing to advance in the organization; or the work might intersect with something that the prospective team member is very interested in. Making such connections can go a long way toward fostering interest in the task at hand.

I once worked with a diversity and inclusion (D&I) professional who was asked to be on a team that was developing operational training processes. I coached a leader to help the D&I specialist understand that shaping operational training is particularly relevant to advancing inclusion in the organization. In this role, she would have the opportunity to insert her expertise in developing training that not only served operational needs, but also influenced operational culture.

Having a D&I professional on a team revamping operational training allowed the team to develop a greater understanding of how operational processes and operational culture could benefit from an inclusive culture. She was able to not only influence operational culture, but also elevate her understanding of how operations worked, what was important to them, and what metrics drove their behaviors.

With this understanding, and with the connections she would make on the team, she gained a much greater ability to drive inclusive cultural practices across the organization. The training content the team developed would go on to influence the behavior of all operations personnel. Once the D&I professional understood the connection and how the team assignment would allow her a much greater level of influence, her enthusiasm increased significantly.

In this case, her leader helped frame the work in a way that helped her realize that operating within a team allowed her to influence the organization far more than she would have had she worked in isolation. Before then, this was her focus and how she saw her role in advancing inclusion. Her deployment to that operational training team opened her eyes to the fact that engaging with the organization on the ground was a far more effective way to not only increase the organizational focus on inclusion, but to actually build it into operational training programs that would influence employees and leaders for a long time to come.

This example typifies not only the framing of important work, but also its reframing. You should monitor the team's perspective on the work over time and reframe its importance as necessary. Consistently keeping the importance of the work front and center is a best practice. And reframing the work from time to time may also be required. Use the same framing skills to reframe work, and link the work to any important outcomes and needs of the organization and its people.

But what if someone isn't interested? You should acknowledge and welcome the idea that not everyone will be interested in all work. This is a not failure on the part of that individual. Too often, people feel like they cannot say they are not interested when they are voluntold to be on a team. The cultural dynamic whereby they are immediately seen as not being a team player should be exorcized from the organizational culture. People need to be allowed, and even encouraged, to honestly express their disinterest. You will have better teams when you do so.

Honoring Important Work

Since important work is the foundation for effective teams, the organization must honor such work. Too often leaders sully the distinction between important and unimportant work and thereby strip the word of its value. We often create teams to execute significant undertakings that require a high level of dedication and discretionary effort. When people believe that they are being bamboozled, they will naturally disengage. I have seen far too many teams become disenchanted when they found that the work was unimportant, the organization changed direction without helping the team understand why, or they were given little autonomy to make decisions and craft solutions. The damage that comes from this can be significant, long-lasting, and widespread.

The outcome is that important work is seen as a flavor of the day. We have all seen programs and initiatives that started with great fanfare only to be half-heartedly embraced and replaced the following year with another initiative that purports to solve the same problem. The organization gets jaded and mistrustful of yet another program, fails to engage, and waits each new program out with the conviction that another is just around the corner.

Being dishonest about the importance of work has a similar impact. Leaders will say, "This work is so critical to our organization," only to later abandon it, underfund it, or not sponsor it effectively. When asked to be on another team the following quarter with similar exhortations of value, the leery team may decide to give the effort exactly what the last team goal required, which is not much.

For teams you lead, you should be upfront about the value of the work, the parameters within which the team will work, and the hoped-for outcome. Articulating these elements is effective in not only orienting the team, but prompting leaders to consider the implications of sending the team into action. Certainly, commitments can be broken, but by deliberately working through this with the team, the moral hazard of willfully breaking trust becomes a powerful tool to help you live up to the commitments you have made. Share these elements with the team:

- **Importance of work:** How is this work actually important? What value-added outcomes will we see? Be specific.
- **Level of sponsorship:** How engaged will the executive be in sponsoring the team?
- **Funding:** What are the funding constraints?
- **Autonomy:** How much autonomy will the team have in charting its course?
- **Commitment to follow up and implementation:** How committed to the output is the organization in terms of follow-through?

I have found that team leaders can be reluctant to deliberately and specifically lay out the obligations they and the organization have to the team. This is sometimes understandable. Conditions and circumstances outside their control can change. They would rather keep things ambiguous and give themselves wiggle room to maneuver in the future. While this may seem wise, the strategy erodes organizational and team trust. People also understand that things change and are willing to accept that their hard work may come to naught. But they will only do so if the organization is honest with them about it. So you should be as honest as you can with your teams.

If you are going to create a team, a real team, then give the team important work and the autonomy, funding, planning, and sponsorship that important work deserves. Frame the work honestly in a way that showcases its value. Link the effort of the team to an outcome that demonstrably improves something in a way that people can be proud of.

In the context of TD organizations, the framing of important work isn't always easy. Safely running a nuclear power plant, caring for sick patients in a hospital, teaching young children, or keeping neighborhoods safe are all clearly and unequivocally important work. In many spaces, however, the direct line to how our work is important, actually important, is less easy to draw.

And yet let me say, the work that TD professionals do, when done well and focused appropriately, is important work. It is not an overstatement to say that TD and L&D professionals are fundamentally in the business of helping leaders and people accomplish their hopes and dreams. That may sound a bit hyperbolic but consider this story. Many years ago, I was involved in creating a development program for union craft members to become supervisors based on their skill and potential. This was not typical in the organization. Seniority was strictly based on time in role and not dependent on skill or potential. The idea of elevating people over others who had more seniority was something the union fought for many years.

From a TD perspective, this situation was not optimal. And after much negotiation, the union was convinced to allow this to happen on a pilot basis. We created a typical leadership development program of the kind that many readers will be familiar with to upskill high-potential skilled-trade workers to become supervisors. After the pilot was complete and our first cohort graduated, one of the new supervisors visited my office. He was a burly and tough man, the kind of no-nonsense guy who had worked turning wrenches all his life. I was surprised by the tears in his eyes as he thanked me for the opportunity to be in the program and to become a supervisor. He had never thought he would be able to do so, and the increased income he received allowed him to get extra help for his special needs child. He was a good leader.

It was at that moment that the importance of the work I had begun to dedicate my life to revealed itself. My work, and the work of the team, directly helped not only this individual to take care of his family, but it also helped the people he would be leading. And, his new role as a leader allowed him to help his direct reports accomplish their hopes and dreams.

It has become a habit of mine to remind myself of that moment when I am frustrated or feeling that the work I am doing isn't making a difference. It makes a difference to people. And that, after all, is the whole point. To make a difference in the world. To make a difference in the lives of the people we work with and with whom we come into contact.

In this sense, it should not be terribly difficult to make that connection in framing the important work that TD professionals do. Whether you are designing an onboarding program, or building a leadership development module, or coaching an executive, you are fundamentally working to make people's lives better. You are directly engaged in helping them become better leaders, better contributors, and better team members. Use this framing when leading or working with a team to consistently focus on the direct and unequivocal connection to the important work you do.

A side effect of this is when people are engaged in important work, they also believe they are important. And when people feel valued, they tend to offer discretionary effort commensurate with the value of that work. Put another way, the perceived importance of the work people do directly correlates to their perception of personal value. And how do people respond when they think that they are important to the accomplishment of something valuable? They engage.

Ensuring Team Autonomy

Autonomy is a critical attribute of important work. This can be challenging for teams, especially if executive leadership does not give them sufficient leeway to develop the problem statement and work through understanding root causes. Executive leaders often create their own problem statements and simply assign the "go-do" to a team. This is not at all optimal for a bunch of reasons. The correct approach is to offer a potential problem statement and then allow the team to investigate whether that problem statement is correct. Allow them to understand whether it addresses the root causes that actually led to whatever gap it's outlining. And give them room to develop effective solutions to close that gap.

Consider This

- The most important teaming skill is the framing of important work. Framing important work links it to something tangible and valuable to the organization, the team, the community, or even the world. It doesn't matter who it is important to, what matters is that the team believes the work is worthy of their time and effort. That it is important enough for them to make sacrifices for.
- Put in the upfront effort to ascertain the importance of the work. Does it meaningfully contribute? Will it create value? Will it solve a problem? Will the effort of the team be worth it?
- Do not lie about the work's importance. This undermines interest in future important work. Honor important work by being honest about the work you do.
- Have conversations with team members around the importance of the work. Do not punish people for saying that they think a particular packet of work is unimportant. In fact, reward behaviors that challenge the importance of work. Build into your culture the conviction that we do not engage in unimportant work.
- Focus on important work and keep it front and center. In team meetings, status calls, and huddles, repeatedly reiterate the importance of the work to maintain alignment and team focus. Team members can, and should, remind each other of why they are doing the work. It may seem like overkill to continually touch base on its importance, but it is too easy for the underlying reason we are engaged in all this effort to get lost.
- Update your perspective on the work as circumstances change, and reframe the work as necessary. If the original framing becomes less important and the underlying reason for the team's existence changes, be sure to reframe to showcase the new importance of the work. For example, if the importance of the work changes from broad organizational impact to smaller departmental impact, that doesn't mean the work is not important, it just means the focus has changed. And that is OK.
- If the work is important, provide autonomy, funding, and sponsorship commensurate with the importance of the work. Allow teams to uncover root causes and develop solutions. Ensuring that the output of the team will be supported and honored drives engagement and effort in current and future teams.

During work with an HR group, I saw an example of the corrosive effect that not allowing sufficient autonomy can have on team effectiveness. As soon as I walked into the meeting room, I could tell something was not right. There were a few team members sitting around a table with forlorn faces. Nick, the team lead, stood at the back of the room, arms crossed. He raised his eyebrows resignedly when I looked over to nod hello.

"What is going on?" I asked him.

He shrugged, "They did not go with our recommendation on the workforce planning project."

"Oh," was all I could say. After a minute of surveying the disappointed faces in the room I asked, "What did they say?"

"Oh, the usual. Budgetary constraints blah blah. Silly. I feel bad for this crew," he said, indicating the team. "They put a lot of work into this and were pretty excited about it. But they rejected most of our recommendations."

I nodded sympathetically, pausing to allow him to continue.

"And of course, now we will have to put in a lot of work to implement something we all know will be pretty useless. I mean the organization has some pretty significant workforce planning problems and we think that our solution would really have made a difference. Would have saved us a lot of money. Now look at them," he nodded ruefully towards the team. "Not fun."

There was not much I could say.

Executives had decided that a new enterprise workforce planning tool was required to track and plan for workforce attrition and to ensure workforce stability and headcount. The new tool was already selected, and a team was put together to investigate its features, recommend the most effective modules, and plan the implementation. After the team worked optimistically and diligently to gather evidence from various stakeholders and do a comprehensive needs analysis, they recommended the modules that would be most effective in tracking headcount, planning for attrition, and coordinating with recruiting. However, those recommendations were modified by executives and a far less effective subset of modules were selected for deployment. The team tried to tell executives that the selected modules would be ineffective to adequately solve for the identified gaps, but to no avail. They were told that the decision had been made and cost considerations would not allow them to purchase the recommended modules.

The outcome here was entirely predictable. Not only had their hard work come to naught, but they now had to put in an enormous amount of work to implement a system that they knew would not be effective. Their work had become unimportant, and the team from that point forward was less effective. Certainly, they went through the motions, but they were less engaged, less innovative, less conscientious, and less motivated. The work had become a chore and the pace and quality of implementation showed it.

Cost considerations are always a factor in decision making, and things can sometimes change. But what approach would have worked better? What if the team had been given the problem statement, a budget within which to work, and latitude to develop the most effective solution? Would that have been a better approach? Of course it would. But for whatever reason, the executives had already decided on the solution, were not clear on the budgetary constraints, and were unwilling to take the team's recommendations on whether they should proceed.

Had the team been given the latitude to understand the potential gap, work through root causes, develop a clear problem statement, and develop effective solutions within reasonable constraints, the organization would have had much better outcomes and a motivated team. The other, and potentially more pernicious outcome, was the erosion of trust that these kinds of incidents engender. The team members will be far less likely to volunteer and engage in future teams knowing that their hard work could easily come to nothing.

Addressing Causes, Not Symptoms

Adopting organizational norms whereby teams are empowered to develop root-cause analysis and design initiatives is more difficult. Cultures that tend toward top-down management styles or that reward people for being the smartest person in the room naturally tend to micromanage teams. This micromanagement deprives teams of their full potential for success. Team leaders and members can mitigate this by pushing back where appropriate, harnessing allies in the organization to influence decision makers, and seeking out team deliverables that simultaneously deliver on goals and address root causes.

For example, an organization tasked a team to develop a process in which internal consultants would help employees create and revise individual development plans. The team devised a strategy to meet that deliverable, as well as helping to mitigate root causes to the problem. They created a program where instead of meeting with employees individually to address their development plans, internal consultants met with the employee and their leader. This allowed internal consultants to meet the deliverable while also upskilling managers on the creation of such plans and to reinforce the ideal, which is that managers are the primary responsible party in developing their employees, not TD.

The team was able to effectively address the root-cause problems they identified, and to execute the tasks that leadership had assigned them. Team leaders and team members can often successfully thread this needle by identifying what is important about the work they are doing and focusing on that as their primary motivator. Of course, the gold standard in creating effective teams is for leadership to create the team and task them with developing root causes and actions. In the absence of this, team leaders and team members can seek out the important work and derive their team satisfaction from that.

Bringing teams into the decision-making process where possible is critically important in how the work and its importance is viewed. A good part of people's perception of their value in an organization or on a team is the sense of autonomy they have in the work they do, why they do it, and how they do it. When you hand a team an outcome and a plan, this diminishes their autonomy and their voice. They have little insight into why they are doing it and how they should go about engaging in solving the problem.

I have been on or observed too many teams that were given an outcome and a plan that didn't address root-cause issues, but instead addressed symptoms. The team often had no ability to address the root cause, even when they understood that the team's task addressed only symptoms, and that their work would have little impact. In such cases, is it any wonder that they did not view the work as important? And if it is not important, how much engagement and passion would that workgroup be able to muster? And when they displayed the negative characteristics of a workgroup in terms of variable engagement and a few members doing most of the work, how frustrated would members of the group and leaders be? When their product is sub-standard, how surprised will they be?

I once worked with an organization that had issues with pipelining and talent development. They were not effectively developing talent and did not have a robust talent pipeline to staff senior leader positions. A hit team was created with orders from above to put together a talent development training program to ensure that leaders had the tools to effectively develop their people. The team dutifully began meeting and working on what the training program might look like. However, they began to struggle, and I was contracted to help them get back on track.

I had an initial meeting with the team, and it was clear they were unhappy. Jordan, the team lead, outlined the team's frustrations. She was a high-potential junior HR leader in the organization known for her enthusiasm and positive demeanor. In that light, her unhappiness and willingness to express it openly was surprising. "Do you think this work is important?" I asked.

"As it currently stands, no," she answered. "We all have a lot on our plates, and being assigned to this team is just another thing. We all think that getting better as leaders is important, but what we are doing here is not useful. We are just reinventing the wheel again and again. And it is a wheel that doesn't work."

I paused for a moment before asking, "Why is developing a new program not useful?"

She shrugged and replied, "Because before we started, we looked at previous training programs to get ideas and realized that basically the same training has been delivered every couple of years for the last 10 years. And clearly none of it worked. Why do they think that doing another one is a good use of our time?"

I sighed, thinking that I had heard this story too many times. "So, what would work?" I asked.

Jordan shrugged. "Maybe if leaders had any consequences at all for failing to develop their people, they would do it. As it stands, leaders have no real reason to develop their people. What we are doing here is silly."

The team had realized that they were working on a symptom, not the cause. And, as such, nothing they did to develop a training program would solve the problem. They, or some other team, would be back at creating a similar program in a couple years when their product similarly failed to move the organization. The team was not a team and would never be. They realized they were not engaged in important work. The organization did not make development a priority for leaders, did not reward leaders for developing employees, and created no accountability when leaders did not develop their people. That was the root cause. Development was not important to leaders.

When this was raised and a recommendation given that a training program would not be effective, what do you think happened? The word from senior leadership was that this was outside the team's scope and they simply needed to deliver the program. Demoralizing. The team had put their brains to work, found a root cause, and would've been ready to develop solutions for that root cause. They then may have become a team, with all the secondary benefits of teaming manifesting to benefit the broader organization. Instead, they were a frustrated and demoralized work group. In the end, they did put together a training program and it was ineffective, just as they knew it would be. I saw Jordan later and asked about the program. She just rolled her eyes and walked away shaking her head.

I see this sort of thing happen all the time. How is this dynamic effective, efficient, and valuable? What opportunity cost are we paying when we not only lose an effective root-cause solution, but also the constellation of secondary benefits that teaming offers the organization? Is it useful to have demoralized people who are now reticent to fully engage with teams because they doubt the importance of their work?

This is a far too typical demonstration of a leadership and organizational failure to actively leverage the voices from below. Building teams that are representative of a vertical slice of your organization allows those who do most of the work in your organization to bring their experience to bear in the identification of root causes, the solving of problems, and the innovation of solutions. Invariably, organizations that leverage these voices and give them sufficient autonomy are more successful in designing workable solutions. Their outputs have a greater chance of organizational adoption and success. Leaders who do not engage with this dynamic often lead demoralized teams who produce suboptimal solutions with variable organizational uptake.

 Consider This

- Give teams autonomy to design their work. Failing to do so deprives the organization of harvesting their innovative capacity. It also tends to drive demoralization and disengagement. Creating teams and not allowing them to uncover root causes and generate accurate problem statements is not an effective use of teams.
- Recognize that teams solve problems. You need to create the circumstances whereby teams have the autonomy to deeply understand the problem and its root causes—and then be able to develop solutions that address those problems. If the work is important, then giving the well-formed team sufficient autonomy increases your chances of getting a workable and effective solution. You might be surprised by what the team comes up with, and may consider moving forward with the recommendation. This may require some amount of leadership courage, but honor this important work by doing so.
- Extend autonomy to the individual. You should ensure each team member has sufficient latitude to solve problems and create solutions. In other words, when team members are given a task, they should be allowed to develop an approach that allows them to work most effectively. This creates a culture of autonomy and allows people and teams to own their work.

Align and Orient the Team Around a Clear Goal

Important work is all well and good, but for teams to most effectively function, that important work needs to be translated into tangible goals and objectives. Teams that do not have discreet and identified work products are not teams; they are just people doing stuff. This is an important distinction that is often lost. I commonly see groups of people who work together without a clear problem statement or objective call themselves a team and act surprised when they do not develop the benefits of teaming. When you cannot clearly see your goal and have no way of measuring your progress toward that goal, team pathologies inevitably begin to manifest. Frustration, disengagement, and destructive conflict are common symptoms of a lack of direction.

Clear objectives require a clear problem statement. For example, developing organizational leadership competence is important work. But in what way? How is lack of leadership competence defined? Why do we have a lack of leadership competence? How do we ensure that we are addressing root causes and not symptoms? Concise and clearly defined problem statements are critical to helping us define a clear and concise goal that addresses root causes and not symptoms. When a problem statement concerning important work is effectively clarified, the team is primed to take action because they understand the problem they are trying to solve and can formulate clear objectives and track their progress toward those objectives accordingly.

The most critical part of developing a plan to address a problem statement is to ensure that you are targeting the root cause of the problem. This may seem obvious, but it is a tragedy that so many teams and leaders do not take this necessary step. Typically, leaders and teams create solutions that address symptoms, not the root cause of the problem.

I once worked with a large production facility where they saw a spike in seal leaks. These leaks caused production to shut down for hours or sometime days while the seals were replaced, which caused significant lost revenue. Leaders quickly settled on a problem statement that technicians were not installing the seals correctly. A team was put together to create the technical training. However, after the training, which came at significant expense, the seals kept leaking. The team was asked to try to figure out what was going on. After some investigating, it was discovered that the seals were being purchased from a different manufacturer and were of lower quality than the seals that were previously used. The solution was to purchase seals from the previous manufacturer. After some months, the seals began to leak again. And again, a team was put together to find out what was going on.

After some digging, the team found that yet a different kind of seal was being used. Perplexed, they began following the chain of how the seals were purchased. Seal specifications were outlined by engineering and entered into the database. Maintenance crews placed purchase orders to buy new seals to resupply their inventory. The purchase order would be sent electronically to purchasing, where they would purchase seals meeting the specifications entered into the database. When the team interviewed purchasing, they asked them why they bought seals from different vendors rather than the one they had used for years. Purchasing replied that they sought out the cheapest seals they could find that met the specifications because their bonus was tied to how much money they saved for the company.

The root cause had been found. It turned out that purchasing was incentivized to get the cheapest seals, not the best seals. In the end, the problem statement had nothing to do with seal installation but was instead tied to fixing the incentives that drove purchasing to buy substandard seals.

This kind of thing happens all the time. Teams, even if they put forth the effort to develop a clear goal and objective, often do not dig deep enough to truly understand the root cause of the problem they are trying to solve. And they end up spending significant time and energy solving symptoms of the problem rather than the root cause.

Problem statement development is a topic that could fill an entire book itself, but briefly speaking, initial problem statements should outline a problem: We are losing money, we are not collaborating effectively, priorities across departments are not aligned. Problem statements necessarily outline a current state versus a different state. "We are not collaborating effectively" implies that in the future, we should be collaborating effectively. The problem statement at this point does not offer solutions, that is for the team to discern. The team can then begin formulating a plan to understand the details and implications of how not collaborating across the organization manifests itself, and then begin to home in on the details of what problems this gap is causing the organization. Further, they can begin to examine these details to ascertain the underlying root cause of the problem. As such, they can reformulate the problem statement in such a way that it focuses the team on a clear and measurable objective.

In the example of the leaky seals, the initial problem statement should have been, "Seals are leaking at an unsustainable rate." The team could then use something like a 5 Whys approach to begin to understand the root cause of those leaks; they could continue to ask "why" at least five times until they found the root cause. Instead, they were given a problem statement and a solution that turned out to be wrong. Much time and energy was wasted using this approach. They would have been better off building a team to meaningfully understand the problem and the root causes that led to the problem, and developing recommendations to solve for it.

TD should help leaders pause, and instead of formulating the plan a priori, they should thoughtfully build a team that has the ability to discern root causes and develop an effective problem statement. TD can help leaders make sure that the objective or goal the team is striving to accomplish is compelling and that the team has the autonomy to develop clear goals grounded in root causes. Team members need to consistently focus on the compelling and important goal. Indeed, the most successful teams I have worked with ensure that the importance of the work and the objective is reiterated frequently.

Consider This

- Resist the temptation to offer a problem and solution to the team. Give teams broad problem statements and allow them to investigate root causes and develop precise problem statements. Effective teaming requires the team to have problem statement development and root-cause analysis skills they can translate into clear and measurable goals and objectives.
- Effective teaming also requires the necessary environment to challenge each other and wrestle with differing perspectives and opinions so that root causes can be found and effective solutions created.

In team meetings, huddles, and updates, the important work should be front and center, and progress toward the goal is prominently displayed. There are many ways to do this, and I have seen a number of teams have some fun with it. One team I worked with created a countdown clock based on milestones achieved. As the team accomplished milestones, the needle moved closer to midnight. These kinds of tools may seem quaint, but they serve a very useful purpose in providing people with a visceral understanding that they are indeed succeeding.

Conclusion

Important work and clear goals are the basis for highly effective teams. It catalyzes teams to take action and engage. It primes people to endure the hardships that engaging in tough challenges requires. Framing the importance of the work and how it will improve some aspect of the organization, community, and participants is a critical first step in building high-performing teams.

Honoring important work requires that we allow our teams to chart their own course, have the autonomy to seek out and formulate root causes, and find solutions to those problems. When these dynamics are in place, we create teams that flourish, challenge effectively, and are fully engaged in identifying problems and innovating novel solutions to those problems. We will further create the far-reaching dynamics of trust and community that can dramatically improve your organization and culture.

CHAPTER 6

Embrace Conflict and Encourage Curiosity

One fundamental barrier to effective teams, and especially to those with diverse personalities and ways of thinking, is that people often annoy one another. In the abstract, we love to talk about how teams populated with people who think differently produce better results. And, when functioning well, they are more likely to innovate and develop more effective solutions. However, the process of integrating different personalities into a team can be perilous. One can easily see the conflict that can occur when different approaches to problem identification and problem solving are brought together. This is one of the primary reasons why important work is so critical to performance.

When considering team personalities and the subsequent conflict that can occur, I have noticed that the more important the work, the more important the team believes the work is, and the more willing they are to express differences and work through those differences. This is worth repeating. When teams are engaged in important work, they are more willing to engage in conflict and work through it. The inverse it also true. When teams are not engaged in important work, they often avoid conflict and do not effectively challenge one another. Poor team conflict is often just as much an outcome of engaging in unimportant work as it is the result of poor conflict management skills. It is easy to see how this dynamic erodes team effectiveness as much as, or possibly more than, lack of conflict management skills.

In the nuclear industry, about every two years power plants have what they call their refuel outage. During this time the plant is shut down, spent fuel is unloaded, and new fuel is loaded into the reactor. Additional maintenance and upgrade work that cannot be done while the reactor is running is also done around the clock. Depending on the scope of work, the reactor will be shut down anywhere from three to six weeks. During that period, the plant is not producing electricity and therefore not making money. Time is of the essence.

To make this possible, an incredible amount of planning goes into preparing for the outage so that all work can be completed safely and in the shortest amount of time. In nuclear power, the outage is like the World Series and Super Bowl all rolled into one. Planning, performance, and perfect execution are paramount. All hands are on deck and everyone involved is ready and willing to do whatever is necessary to ensure the outage is done safely and on time. When done well, it is a ballet with thousands of workers executing work choreographed down to the minute. The teamwork and execution are a beautiful thing to watch. In the nuclear industry, this is truly important work. And everyone knows it.

Observing team conflict in this environment is illuminating. Due to the overwhelming importance of the work, nuclear professionals at the best sites willingly, actively, and forcefully engage in conflict. Since any error or missed opportunity can derail the success of the outage, team members simply cannot remain silent. Success literally depends on the willingness of every individual—from the trade level up to the site vice president—to challenge one another. The importance of the work and the consequences of failure automatically drive conflict and challenges. The most successful sites allow the importance of the work to drive the organization to embrace and encourage challenge at all levels.

In the context of important work, this observation makes sense. The dynamic is very much like videos I've seen where someone is trapped under a car after a traffic accident and bystanders quickly and spontaneously gather to get the car off the unfortunate victim. There is no planning, no team builds, no discussion of values, no discussion of roles.

The work is obvious, critically important, and time is of the essence. The bystanders immediately begin working together to move the car.

In an instant, they are a team. Everyone wants to do whatever is needed to save the victim. And while this example is a hyperbolic microcosm of teamwork, it is also illustrative of how humans are wired to come together to do important work. When work is important, people are not only willing, but eager to engage. Important work activates that natural tendency, and good leaders leverage it to solve problems and innovate solutions.

This creates an environment where team members naturally wish to offer their perspective and challenge, but because the stakes are high, it can also drive leadership behaviors that inhibit challenge and perspective sharing. Since leaders will be held accountable to failure, they can easily tend toward micromanaging and authoritarian leadership styles. They shut down dissent, challenge, and perspective sharing in an effort to stave off errors, mistakes, and failure. However, as we've discussed, challenge and actively wrestling with different ideas almost inevitably leads us to better outcomes. The efforts of leaders to exact total control to avoid failure ironically make failure more likely.

And what about the impact of micromanaging and authoritarian leadership styles on team dynamics? The effort of leaders to exact control not only diminishes challenge and the formulation of the best approach, but it also diminishes team autonomy, team ownership, and therefore team morale. It promotes disengagement, disaffection, and destructive conflict. When the team has little autonomy, little ownership, no ability to make decisions, and therefore no ability to meaningfully engage in the important work, it will inevitably engage in destructive conflict. All the pathologies of ineffective teams will become evident. Petty jealousies, information withholding, territorialism, gossip, and political maneuvering all begin to rear their ugly heads. It is a paradoxical truth that one of the best ways to inhibit destructive conflict of this kind is to promote and demand challenge and dissent. When allowed and encouraged to engage in constructive conflict, teams will be less likely to engage in destructive conflict.

It is critical for team leaders to understand this dynamic. Time and again I work with leaders who are confused as to why their teams engage in this kind of destructive conflict. Sometimes they begin to understand that their own leadership behaviors are driving that behavior, and sometimes they do not. It requires a reasonable level of confidence in yourself and your leadership style to actively solicit conflict and challenge, to willingly and openly admit that you do not have all the answers—to embrace the idea that there may be others that have a better idea or solution. That is, after all, why the team exists in the first place; to get other perspectives. But too many leaders are not confident enough to release control, to adopt a posture where they do not have all the answers—to allow the team to work.

In regular nuclear online operations, the work is important—but it isn't as important as work during the outage. As a result, conflict tends to be less constructive. Team pathologies are far more prevalent in online work than they are in outage work. The important work of the outage drives more effective team behaviors, toxic leadership styles notwithstanding. When the work is important, people want to challenge constructively because the outcome is important to them. When the work isn't important to people, they are apathetic to the outcome and often simply go along to get along. Solutions are harder to find, engagement is lackluster, and outcomes are less than they could be.

I offer the admittedly extreme example of the nuclear industry to yet again relate how the importance of work is critical to high-functioning teams. When leaders effectively relate the importance of work and allow teams to make decisions and own the work, team conflict is much more likely to be fruitful and constructive. Different personalities that would otherwise annoy one another tend to understand the value that they contribute to successfully engaging in the important work and producing successful outcomes. Definitionally, people deeply care about important work. Their willingness to contribute discretionary effort, engage in challenge and conflict, and embrace differences are all enhanced because they deeply care about the outcome.

Consider This

- Important work activates engagement. In many ways, engagement can be measured by the level of conflict and challenge one sees in how a team works together. Constructive conflict tends to inhibit destructive conflict.
- Given the harm that destructive conflict can do to teams, actively work to encourage constructive conflict and build team skills to that end.
- Recognize that your leadership style can create a climate of either constructive conflict or destructive conflict. Temper your desire to control the work. Enlist others to monitor your approach to ensure you are leveraging the innovative capacity of your teams and actively encouraging constructive conflict.

Curiosity Is the Key to Constructive Conflict

Important work breeds constructive conflict. When people are willing to wrestle with ideas, it typically means they care. That is a good thing. But knowing how to effectively engage in conflict and challenge is a skill that team members need to be good at. Important work can also breed a level of intensity that can easily translate into raised voices, hurt feelings, and passive-aggressive (or openly aggressive) behavior. The primary key to avoiding and resolving destructive conflict is curiosity. It is a team norm that leaders must instill, and that team members must embrace. Curiosity is the lubricant that allows good teams to vigorously challenge one another and collectively drive toward the best solution.

In my work with high-performing teams, I often see conflict arise when people are wedded to a particular position or event. For example, one person thinks the leadership development program should be facilitated by leaders so that they can have effective ownership of the message to participants, but another person thinks the program should be facilitated by experienced trainers so the content can be most effectively conveyed. The two positions are at odds, and they both have a reasonable argument as to why theirs is the best solution. But why do they hold these positions? What outcomes are they each trying to achieve? One wishes for the participants to most effectively internalize the contents of the program. The other wishes for leaders to own the content so participants can see, and the organization can telegraph, that development is a leadership function. The two team members who are at odds can either continue to press for the position they want and remain at odds until a leader breaks the logjam and makes the final decision, or they can explore together what outcomes they are trying to accomplish.

In such cases, curiosity is the key. If each team member is genuinely curious about the motivations, thought processes, and needs of the other, they can begin a dialogue that helps them better understand those needs, and potentially design a solution that meets them. At the very least, even if they cannot find a solution that meets both their needs, they will come away with a better understanding of why the other person feels the way they do. With genuine curiosity, they may learn something that they didn't know before. They may even change their minds. In this light, curiosity becomes a skill as much as it is a feeling. We can get better at demonstrating curiosity by implementing some rules and behavioral norms around how we approach disagreement and conflict.

"Tell Me More"

In a curious culture, the most important words are "tell me more." In any disagreement, that should always be the response. Always. "Tell me more" means that you are interested and you value the other person's perspective and experience. After all, if you didn't value their opinion, you wouldn't ask. "Tell me more" broadcasts that you care enough about the other person to hear them out, and to understand their motivations and concerns. "Tell me more" means you are willing to learn and update your view given information you might not have had or a perspective you might not have considered. "Tell me more" significantly contributes to creating the shared purpose and community that we see when effectively teaming—a shared sense of purpose and community that drives engagement, commitment, and discretionary work.

Had our two team members started their dialogue with "tell me more," they would have been able to decipher the other's motivations and underlying thought processes. They would have been able to see that their opinions were offered in the spirit of furthering the goals of the team, and they might have been able to develop a solution that effectively taught the content and telegraphed leadership ownership of the material. Once they had this discussion, the two team members agreed on a solution where leaders and TD professionals would codesign and facilitate the content. This satisfied the outcomes they were both interested in. Curiosity and deploying "tell me more" immediately allowed them to begin to solve for an outcome that addressed all their concerns.

In working with teams over the years, I have seen the deployment of curiosity and "tell me more" head off more destructive conflict than I can count. Upon adopting this methodology, teams that frequently butted heads in ineffective ways transformed into teams that engaged in constructive conflict and challenge. The frequency of destructive conflict decreased, while the frequency of constructive challenge increased. The quality of solutions improved, and their time to deployment fell. The team developed greater levels of purpose and community and was more likely to presuppose that their teammates were acting in the best interests of the team.

Here are some questions and statements that may help you build a curiosity culture. You can use these as a script if you'd like. It may seem awkward at first, but after some consistent use, it will feel weird if you don't operate this way. Try saying:

- Tell me more.
- What outcome are you looking for?
- What concerns you about this solution?
- This is what I think and here is my thought process.
- What do you think about that?
- What are the flaws in my thinking?

The Interview Format

A formal way to implement a curiosity and tell-me-more culture is to adopt a communication style that mimics the interview format. This simply involves using the interview techniques one might see and hear on a long-form talk show or podcast—think Larry King. Place yourself in the position of the interviewer with the intention of finding out all there is to know about a person or topic. The key is that interviewers are not in the business of trying to win. They are in the business of gathering information. And that is exactly what a curiosity culture looks like in practice. The interview format requires team members to ask questions rather than state opinions. It forces people to hold off on making judgements and instead to probe for more information and clarity.

The rules of this game are relatively simple—remain curious throughout the conversation. The interviewer's job is to solicit valid information, for example facts, opinions, or even feelings. Much like a talk show host, they should remain neutral when gathering information, make no judgement, and attempt no argument. The interviewer's internal dialogue must be centered on the idea that "I am open to the possibility that I do not have all of the relevant information, and I may be incorrect in my judgements and opinions."

This inner monologue, or mantra of sorts, allows us to better listen and integrate alternate ideas and information. It helps us listen to understand rather than listen to reply by placing the focus on the other and not on ourselves. The interview ensures that team members feel heard. Remember, most team members do not necessarily need all their opinions and recommendations be followed. They simply wish to be heard and for their thoughts and opinions to be considered. It is in the hearing that people feel valued. If someone is willing to take the time to fully hear someone out and solicit their perspectives and opinions, that act represents a significant investment of time and energy. The act of investing this time and energy to solicit information is, in effect, an investment in that person. This is powerful.

The interview serves two purposes. It is a facet of curiosity culture and a more formal way to engage in "tell me more" dialogue. It also serves to solicit information, perspectives, and opinions so that we can make better decisions. It is also a powerful tool to demonstrate that we value our teammates. When people feel like they are valuable members of a winning team, they are far more likely to have higher levels of engagement and offer greater levels of discretionary effort. Certainly, there is a time to state opinions. Certainly, there is a time to challenge, as we have seen. But prior to the statement of opinions and offering challenge, it is critical that we gather information.

 Consider This
- Create a curiosity culture that always answers conflict with "tell me more."
- Look for outcomes that meet the needs of all—do not focus on a particular action.
- Adopt the interview format as a means to formally model curiosity.

Conclusion

TD professionals can integrate this practice into how their teams, and the teams of those they consult with, work. The adoption of a curiosity culture and use of "tell me more" dialogue techniques can be rather ambiguous at first. They may even seem more aspirational than implementable. The interview models curiosity culture in a way that, over time, inspires people to begin to integrate its precepts into how they regularly interact with one another. And as we have discussed, when teams create mechanisms that actually work, those tools and practices often bleed into other parts of the business as team members bring those useful ideas with them.

Leaders and team members need to commit to a curiosity culture and "tell me more" conflict management style that they reinforce as the primary mechanism of dialogue, problem solving, and conflict resolution. Important work primes us for conflict. When people deeply care about the work, they are more likely to wrestle with ideas and advocate for solutions that they think will most effectively accomplish the important work. Curiosity and "tell me more" dialogue not only allows us to build effective solutions, but also helps mitigate the kind of destructive conflict that passionate engagement in important work can engender. Curiosity is the key to creating a fertile ground for another component of teaming that many teams shy away from, but that is critical for success: challenge.

CHAPTER 7

Engage in Challenge

The value of challenge cannot be overstated. Most people are not very good with challenge. However, given its importance in how teams function and the benefit constructive challenge can have on an organization, I think it behooves us to define the term. When I talk about challenge, I am referring to the ability of people to actively and vocally disagree and creating the conditions necessary for what I will call equanimous disagreement to take place. Organizations that cannot disagree, that cannot openly discuss and air different perspectives, opinions, and approaches, are doomed. Given how important this organizational dynamic is, and how bad people often are at engaging in it, it is interesting that organizations do not give more focus to building this skill set.

Let me make this observation: After working with hundreds of teams and organizations over the years, if there is one core teamwork skill that predicts success, it is the ability to constructively challenge one another. Certainly, there are preconditions to creating a culture where constructive challenge is the norm, such as engaging in important work and adopting a curiosity culture, but beyond that, effective challenge is the most important attribute teams can develop.

Challenge Culture

Building challenge as a cultural attribute of your team and organization is a best and critical practice. I have worked in several industries in my career, and most of them were very different in their cultural makeup. What I have seen is that in highly risk-averse organizations where the consequences of failure or mistakes are high, they generally develop a keen sense of challenge. They become very good at disagreeing and considering different opinions. When the stakes are high, teams and organizations cannot afford to make a mistake. I have spent a good deal of time in the nuclear industry, and they have developed this skill very well. In fact, as an industry they have perfected the art of challenge. And this makes perfect sense. Their business priority, perfect execution, drives the impetus to challenge. Woe to the leader who makes a decision without getting challenge and input from others and then making a mistake. The penalty for such a mistake is severe. And so, challenge is built into how the organization functions.

Most organizations don't have the impetus to develop challenge in the way the nuclear industry or the airline industry has, since they lack places where mistakes could literally lead to disaster. But I wish they did. Their team outcomes would be considerably better. Challenge is the crucible within which decisions are fired and tempered. Without effective challenge, we are not leveraging the perspective of others and we are, in effect, relying on the wisdom of a single individual or groupthink to weigh the pros and cons, to think about what could go wrong, to anticipate roadblocks, and to decipher the best approach. Organizations and teams that develop this skill argue about decisions, and each person is open to the possibility that they could be wrong or have insufficient data. Collectively they triangulate on an approach that takes into account all available information and perspectives. Challenge is a powerful decision-making tool. In fact, it is the best.

To be fair, challenge does take longer than a single individual making a decision. And this is one of the roadblocks that I have seen. People and organizations want decisions, and they often want them made quickly. Engaging teams in challenge can be time-consuming. Additionally, depending on the criticality of a situation, a quick decision may be necessary. But usually, this is not the case. In non-time sensitive decisions, purposefully engaging in challenge is the most effective course of action.

Challenge for Engagement

A secondary but important benefit of challenge is creating an environment of inclusion and personal value. When people are given the opportunity to not only express an opinion, but also to argue for it, they gain a sense of value. In other words, if my opinion is sought after and considered, it shows that my opinion is worth listening to and considering. People want to be heard and have their opinions considered; they want to be seen as someone with the expertise and perspective worth listening to in the first place. Most people do not require that their recommendation be followed exactly, they simply want to be heard and given a fair consideration. When teams engage in effective constructive challenge, they create a sense of value for those on the team. The very act of challenging, and having that challenge be meaningfully heard, enhances their sense of value on the team. Now, consider the implications of a challenge or the voicing of an alternate opinion that is immediately shot down. To what extent does this minimize their perception of value on the team?

As a team leader, one of your jobs is to invite challenge and seek out people who disagree with you. This is not always an easy task. It requires some level of professional confidence that recognizes that you may not have all the right answers or relevant information. Some people are very concerned about having all the right answers or being the smartest person on the team. Abandon that perspective. You are almost never the smartest person on the team in all things, all the time. And even if you are, you simply cannot have all relevant information related to the topic at hand. Your job as a leader or team member is to leave your ego at the door and solicit different ideas, even if they undercut your perspective or opinion. This obviously requires a level of humility that can be difficult to muster. But you must do so if you want to get to the best decision.

The culture within which you work can also enhance your eagerness to be the smartest person in the room. Some cultures reward a posture of confidence, and even arrogance, over a posture of humility. This kind of culture tends toward toxicity for a bunch of reasons, not the least of which is that it diminishes the ability of people to voice different opinions. It also tends to diminish morale and the sense of value people have on the team. Even if you are the smartest person in the room, that doesn't necessarily mean that you always have to win.

Thinking that you are the smartest person in the room also presupposes that you have all relevant information, and that you won't make a mistake. However, the very fact that you believe that you are immune to making mistakes indicates that you are not wise. Wisdom is far more indicative of leadership and team-member potential than intellect. Your ability to recognize the value that different perspectives bring to a decision is one of your primary leadership and team-member skills. Your ability to recognize that engaging people in decision making generates higher levels of team engagement. Even if you are the smartest person in the room, and do have all the answers, you might consider redirecting your intellect toward figuring out how you can let others come up with the great idea that you currently hold. Great team leaders and members want their team to succeed, grow, and feel valued. They are dedicated to the idea that one of their jobs is to work to not only solve organizational challenges, but also to elevate those on their team.

Challenge as a Litmus Test of Team Engagement

A challenge culture can also be a good litmus test for levels of engagement on your team. When I observe teams, I am on the lookout for how often and how many of the members engage, specifically in challenge. When I see teams with low levels of challenge, that usually translates to low levels of engagement. There are a couple of reasons for this. When there is no challenge, it is often because of fear or disinterest.

Fear is a primary killer of a functional challenge culture. This usually relates to what we were talking about in the previous section. Team members are afraid to challenge or disagree because they are avoiding some negative outcome. For example, a leader or team member explicitly, or implicitly, ridicules the perspective of another team member, or otherwise diminishes their contribution. Sometimes leaders or team members straight-up punish team members for offering a different opinion or perspective. It would be an understatement to say that this is a suboptimal team environment.

Another reason I see lack of challenge and disagreement is just plain old disinterest. If team members do not care about the team, the work, or the outcome, they will check out of the conversation. To them, it doesn't matter what decisions are made because the work doesn't fundamentally matter. Again, we are brought back to the criticality of important work. If someone doesn't believe the work is important, then they will downgrade it in their personal importance matrix and dedicate little of their time and energy toward it. To be clear, the work may be important, but for whatever reason it is not to that individual.

Team leaders and team members should be on the lookout for lack of challenge and investigate whether it is driven by fear or disinterest. Both are toxic to the functioning of the team and can significantly diminish the power of a challenge culture.

If you ascertain that lack of challenge is driven by fear, you must work to eliminate it. Edward Deming's words, "Eliminate fear from the organization," echo to us once again. When a challenge culture is effectively built, the team itself can moderate team member actions or words that contribute to fear. It can, and should, be a norm to frown upon minimizing team member contributions, opinions, perspectives, and disagreements. Team members should speak out in instances where opinions are ridiculed or minimized. Of course, this is not to say that we cannot disagree with a disagreement. We should say we disagree when we disagree. But ridicule and shame have no place in a functioning challenge culture.

If disengagement is the result of disinterest and apathy, then team leaders and team members need to have tough conversations about the importance of the work and decide whether it is actually important. If it is not, then be honest about it. If the work is important, team leaders and members can attempt to engage with recalcitrant members to demonstrate the importance of the work. If there are individuals who cannot effectively function on any team, then you have a different problem that may be best addressed though your performance management tools.

More Challenges to Challenge

We are naturally predisposed to maintain harmonious relationships. People don't generally want to argue with others, have awkward relationships, or hurt other people's feelings. Contrary to what we see on the news, most people do not want to cause harm to others—either physically or psychologically. People are wired for community; it is what human beings do. We do not naturally wish to cause harm to people and will often avoid doing so absent a compelling personal interest. There will always be those who are just jerks, but they are the exception.

Our predisposition to harmony can actually inhibit the creation of an effective challenge culture. In fact, I will go so far as to say that in my experience, teams that always agree are almost never great teams. In the absence of fear or apathy, the general reticence to disagree that many people have often leads them to simply go along to get along. It is important to recognize this dynamic and ensure that the team doesn't always agree. The team must be willing and able to voice disagreement. Some may object, claming that disagreement points to a team that is not functioning well. This sentiment is understandable but isn't true. If you are engaged in important work, if people are invested in the work and believe the outputs of the team are critical to success, and if they are passionate about the outcomes, then they will disagree. If you find no disagreement, then you might consider whether you are really engaged in important work.

Creating a Challenge Culture

Given the potential roadblocks to creating a challenge culture, it is important that leaders and teams are purposeful about doing so. As we've seen, a couple of components are needed: important work and the elimination of fear. Once you've established that you are engaged in important work, the primary roadblocks are fear cultures and a natural reticence to engage in challenge. When I work with teams, they typically recognize this and make solemn pronouncements that they will engage in challenge. And then, of course, they don't. Certainly, they start with good intentions, but over time those intentions are lost in the day-to-day and they begin to gravitate to their previous norms. The cultural immune system kicks in and attempts to push people back into established patterns of behavior.

To anyone who has worked with or on teams, this is probably a familiar pattern. People naturally gravitate toward the comfort of the status quo, so building a process to overcome this inertia is essential. The remedy is simply to demand challenge. Leaders can set up challenge gates to ensure that people have the opportunity, or are even required, to disagree. It is effective to assign someone to be a designated challenger, whose job it is to find fault with whatever decisions the team comes up with. Over time, challenge is normalized, and the team will notice when it is absent. Building a process like this may seem a bit silly. And in the beginning, it can feel that way. But like any habit, it is essential to just do it over and over again until it becomes natural. The benefits of a challenge culture are far too great to not pay purposeful attention to its creation.

Talent development professionals have a significant role to play here, not only in helping leaders recognize the power of a challenge culture, but also in helping them understand the dynamics necessary to create one. As we saw earlier in the HR team that didn't challenge one another, their outcomes were not that great. They didn't seek out root causes and they didn't purposefully say, "Let's figure out why this may be a dumb idea." The lack of challenge disabled their ability to be an effective and valuable team.

Leaders need to purposefully invite and demand challenge. Talent development professionals can coach leaders on this and help them recognize when the organization is falling back into old habits. You can help leaders see when the team is beginning to eschew challenge because it is often easier to defer disagreement. You can help teams and leaders create defined processes that not only encourage challenge but require it. While important work encourages challenge, you can help ensure that it is constructive and that teams continue to engage in it.

Challenge Cannot Be Seen as Bad

Lastly, I will add a note to the concept of challenge that is critically important: Challenge cannot be seen as negative. When challenge arises, your default reaction cannot be that the challenger isn't a team player. This dynamic is endemic in most organizations. And it is toxic. It directly contributes to the fear culture that we talked about earlier. Fear cultures are not created solely by singularly toxic people who are rude and angry jerks.

Thankfully, that kind of behavior is becoming less and less tolerated. However, fear cultures can just as easily be created by less outwardly rude behavior. Team members, and especially team leaders, must purposefully and vocally insist that disagreement is welcomed and rewarded. In the absence of reward for challenge, or if challenge is punished, people will simply stop challenging. Leaders will divorce themselves from the benefits of diverse teams and the multiplicity of perspectives that challenge brings. The old saying, "Leaders who don't listen will eventually be surrounded by people who have nothing to say" applies here. People quickly learn that asking questions and challenging is not worth the pain.

This is tough for many leaders, who often have an agenda or a predesigned plan or outcome that they are working toward. And for a number of reasons, many leaders are not transparent about that plan or outcome.

Or, if they articulate the plan or outcome, they do so in a way that brooks no disagreement. Sometimes this is because leaders are driven by something other than what is best for the organization and the team. Often, as we've seen, leaders need to be the smartest person in the room and have all the answers. Sometimes, they need to be seen as the person who thought up that great idea and drove it to execution as they angle for their next promotion. These ego-driven behaviors are toxic to team cohesion and excellence. They disenfranchise the team from engaging in decision making, minimize its autonomy, and drive dissatisfaction that manifests as low morale. Leaders must be vigilant about their reasons for not allowing the team to decide what they will do and how they will do it.

To be fair, dictating an outcome and a plan is sometimes necessary. Sometimes the organization at a higher level has dictated an outcome or plan that the team has to carry out. But too often organizations build cultures where this is the norm—where teams are given an outcome and a plan that they simply have to carry out. This norm can diminish the effectiveness and adoption of challenge culture in that people begin to believe they have no voice and no way to influence the trajectory of their work and the work of the team. And so, why bother disagreeing and challenging? Indeed, this also diminishes the many secondary benefits of teaming that can have wide and positive effects for the organization. Teams and team leaders must be vigilant about this dynamic.

The short answer in how to avoid all of this is the creation of a challenge culture, the purposeful divestment of ego from leaders' decision making, and the empowerment of teams to actually solve problems and innovate solutions. Talent development professionals and leaders are positioned to ensure that this happens. Creating processes that require challenge is an effective way to integrate it into the organization and your teams. Building a process for your team that demands challenge insulates people from their natural reticence to challenge, as well as alleviates the sense that challenge may not be appreciated. Once such processes are created, over time this simply becomes how we do business, and the absence of challenge is seen as weird. If creating such a formalized process feels forced, or even foolish, that is good evidence that a process is necessary.

 Consider This

- A primary teaming skill is generating the willingness and cultural imperative that challenge is valued and necessary, and then learning to effectively challenge one another in ways that drive progress toward team goals.
- Monitor the team's willingness to challenge. Creating purposeful processes that drive challenge is an area where everyone can contribute. Hold the team accountable for using those processes. Ensure that curiosity is the primary mental model that allows challenge and constructive conflict to happen. Reward challenge behaviors.
- When challenge is not seen, use that as a marker to check for engagement and fear. Reframe the importance of the work as needed and monitor for behaviors that drive people to remain silent.

Conclusion

Effective challenge is at the heart of any successful, high-performing team. The ability of team members to effectively disagree about the important work they are engaged in is one of the primary indicators of successful teams. As we've seen, it is through wrestling with different perspectives and ideas that teams come to the most effective solutions to the problems they face. And it is through this iterative process of curiosity and challenge that teams navigate a sometimes winding path to success. Some problems are relatively easy to diagnose and solve. Others are much more difficult. In fact, it may be that the more important the work is, the more difficult it is to effectively solve. And, of course, that is one of the main reasons we build teams—to solve our most difficult problems. It is in engaging in the process of curiosity and challenge while solving important problems that, in the end, is the very thing that leads to the most benefit for our organization: the development of trust and community that lives on far after the team is disbanded.

CHAPTER 8
Build Trust

Trust is one of the most important secondary outcomes of team effectiveness. It is like the holy grail of high-performing teams. But, trust is not something that you can dictate or make happen. It is an outcome of people struggling together to accomplish truly important work. Trust is a result.

Teams that trust one another, whose members truly believe that they have each other's backs, are seen as valuable, and are able to be open and honest with one another, and leave their egos at the door, are much more likely to be highly effective. This is obvious because the inverse is so clearly true. Teams of people who distrust one another, are afraid that their teammates do not have their backs, do not feel valuable, and are continually guarded around one another lest a teammate pounce on a perceived weakness or momentary lapse are much more likely to be ineffective. We've all been on such teams, and they are miserable.

I am often asked how to build trust on teams. My answer is often not what leaders, TD professionals, and individual team members want to hear. Trust is not created through team-building exercises and trust falls. It is created by fits and starts through struggling together to accomplish something important. That is the magic formula, such as it is.

In such circumstances, all ego is stripped away and we are laid bare before our peers. This is a scary proposition to most people. There is some undercurrent in most of us that if we are revealed as we actually are, if the mask that we all wear every day is removed, people will see our true selves. They will see that we do not have all the answers, that we can be wrong, and that we are sometimes uncertain and don't quite know what to do. And, as such, we worry will be rejected. Yet, that is precisely what needs to happen, and what inevitably happens when we really struggle together as a team to accomplish truly important work.

Moving Beyond Talking About Trust

For leaders and TD professionals, understanding this dynamic leads us to the conclusion that we must create the conditions where true trust and vulnerability is possible. Team builds and the like do not have the power to do this. Only the time, work, and the struggle itself can force us to lay down our ego and stand exposed with our team as true teammates.

If you want teamwork, then give the team work. It's a phrase I love and have used for years, and it is a fundamental secret for building teams and team trust. It is one of those phrases that is so obviously true as to almost not bear mentioning. But wade through the confusion of team effectiveness characteristics, assessments, and models and you finally get to the whole point—teams do important work together and it is through the effort of doing that work that trust is built and teams become effective.

I often have organizations ask me to do team building and training to build trust and cohesion. The usual course of events goes something like this: There's possibly an assessment like the DiSC or MBTI to get people to think about their differences and how they can work better together. There is usually some kind of off-site event or retreat in which we talk about teamwork, vision, and the characteristics of good teams. There may be role playing or some other activity to practice working together or build trust. The goal, of course, is to create a team, or at least create the conditions whereby an effective team might form.

In the end, team-building activities usually seem like a reasonable thing to do. Plus, what harm could come by doing them? But I am not sure there is any quantitative evidence that they will result in better team performance. Would the outcomes have been very different if we hadn't done the team building? I have seen some anecdotal evidence that these activities can actually diminish the effectiveness of teams. They certainly do not have the power to create trust—that is built through the collective execution of important work.

I will posit that we spend too much time thinking about the team and not enough time working as a team. We can talk about the team all day long, but in the end, it is the work that energizes the team. And it is success in the execution of that work that makes the team great. Without success, it is hard to say if the team was great or engaged in successful teamwork. Operational success, then, defines team success. And successful teams are, almost by definition, happy teams.

What I am advocating is that instead of spending lots of time and money on team-building activities, let the important work the team needs to accomplish be the team-building activity. Let that work and the struggle required to advance it be the arena where trust is built and people are finally forced to simply be who they are.

To accomplish this, you should, first of all, be patient. You might have the understandable urge to imbue teams with high levels of trust very quickly. Leaders often express frustration when their teams do not exhibit the characteristics of high-performing teams within a couple of weeks. But these characteristics take time to develop. Team builds and orientation events designed to kick-start trust and team effectiveness should focus on designing and aligning on team mechanics rather than explicitly building trust. Useful questions for the team might include:

- What is the vision of the team?
- Why is this work important?
- What are the values and norms we will embrace, such as curiosity and challenge?
- How will work be distributed?

This is actual work that the team can do to begin aligning the trajectory of the team. Beyond that, they should quickly engage in the actual work, utilizing the concepts of team leadership such as effective distribution of work, curiosity, and effective challenge. Always remember that trust is an outcome of shared struggle and purpose, not a prerequisite.

Being Trustworthy

To foster trust, be trustworthy. When leaders ask me how to foster trust, that is my standard answer. And leaders often respond with an eyeroll. Leaders and team members know that high-performing teams have a high level of trust; and it is a lack of trust that frustrates work groups who yearn for a space where they can simply be themselves, offer their honest opinion, and be valued for it.

Yet despite the obviousness of "if you want trust, be trustworthy," people often are not actually trustworthy, failing to act in a way that lives up to the truth embedded in the phrase.

Perhaps people have such a hard time with being trustworthy because they have not defined the attributes of trustworthiness or what it really means to tell the truth and the implications of not telling the truth and breaking trust. I will say that brazen untrustworthiness is pretty easy to identify. But most people do not engage in the brazen and elicit breaking of trust. Most people do it in far subtler ways that do far more damage to your organization.

There is something existential about trust and the breaking of trust on a team through dishonesty or lying. Nothing good comes from a lie. In a very real way, lies are the brick and mortar of pain in the world. For every lie told, even if you cannot perceive it and no matter your intent, it damages you, the world, your organization, and your team in some way.

To be clear, it is easy to lie, and it is often convenient to lie. It can seem advantageous to lie if it can get us what we want or protect what we have. And after all, we often have such good reasons to lie. We may think it is better for morale if our people don't know the truth. We may not want to hurt anyone's feelings. And we are, after all, good people. There are a million rationalizations and justifications that we can easily conjure up to lie.

However, nothing erodes an organization like lies. If you want to disengage people, tell them lies. If you want to ensure that cynicism and distrust flourish on your team, tell them lies. If you want to ensure that people are not giving you their best effort and working hard to ensure your organization thrives, tell them lies. If you want people to leave, tell them lies. And make no mistake, you don't have to tell big lies. Small lies will suffice—they can do much damage. They damage your credibility as a team leader or member, they encourage distrust from every quarter, they breed resentment and disengagement, and they cause people to stop contributing to whatever you are trying to accomplish. The very short answer to how to create trust on a team is to never tell a lie.

Bald-faced lying is the most obvious form of untruth. But obviously, anything that breaks trust is corrosive to the establishment and maintenance of trust. Not living up to our commitments, speaking behind people's backs, withholding information, leveraging others for personal advancement, taking credit for other people's work, playing politics, showing favoritism: these are all forms of dishonesty. Actions that fit this broader definition of lying corrode team effectiveness by sowing mistrust and doubt among team members. They not only prevent effective challenge but also, and perhaps most importantly, inhibit the creation of community and belonging that fundamentally fuels the loyalty that makes teams truly effective.

The first step to establishing trust is to be honest, even if that undermines what you think your interests are. You may think that trying to sell unimportant work to fool people into thinking it is important, and thereby gain some initial engagement, is a good idea. You may think that not giving people honest feedback on their performance to avoid hurt feelings is a good idea. These are unequivocally bad ideas. The skill in being honest is to simply embrace courage and integrity. Develop and leverage your curiosity and challenging skills to frame your honesty in ways that are constructive. But be honest about your intentions, your purposes, and your goals.

You can work to foster an environment where people have license to be honest by rewarding honest behavior and discouraging dishonest behavior. You should be on the lookout for dishonesty and punish it when your see it. Favoritism, politicking, and information withholding are all examples of dishonesty that should trigger direct coaching.

The development of a challenge culture is also helpful in rooting out such behaviors. In a well-formed challenge culture, team members have license to challenge one another's behaviors and ask questions. When this happens, you should be quick to reward teams that hold each other accountable and challenge behaviors that erode team performance. This is tough work, and you need to provide rewards to drive it. In fact, challenging each other is just another form of being trustworthy. In that light, not providing critical feedback and calling out bad behaviors is itself a form of dishonesty.

Trust is an outcome of teams struggling together to accomplish important work. Trust and vulnerability are the result of people being placed in a situation where they must rely on one another to survive. Vulnerability is the result of people not being able to hide their true selves. In the crucible of challenge and suffering, people are revealed for who they actually are, and what they can contribute despite their flaws. In the end, they are valued by the team for those flaws. There are no shortcuts to trust. It is the outcome of the struggle, not a prerequisite.

 Consider This

- Being trustworthy is a brave act. It requires that you sublimate your own desires for the good of the organization and team in the hope that all will benefit from it. Like any skill, it requires practice. You must have faith that the outcome of being trustworthy, over time, is greater than the outcome of being dishonest. There are a million reasons to be dishonest and the draw to take those shortcuts can be strong. But in the end, it damages the ability of the team to generate trust. Teams without trust are not effective. And it always damages the individual, even if they cannot perceive it.
- Holding each other accountable in the context of curiosity and challenge are ways you can reduce dishonest behavior. You should be intolerant of untrustworthy behaviors because they erode team cohesion. Do not reward these behaviors or ignore them. They will prevent the team from becoming a team.
- Trust is an outcome of the shared struggle to accomplish something important. Being trustworthy is the first and possibly the most important contribution you can offer to whatever team you are on. Without being trustworthy, it is impossible to generate the team trust that shared struggle generates, and that everyone on great teams wishes to partake in.

Identifying Interest

An important, but overlooked, component of trust is in team selection as it relates to interest in the work. You should select those who are actually interested in the work you are engaging in. Important work doesn't always generate interest. People's personalities, perspectives, and experiences influence the level of interest they have in any given situation. If we want to generate high levels of engagement, it behooves us to consider the level of interest of prospective team members. We've touched on this before, but it is a critical point.

As we've said, we should not be in the business of holding team members hostage to work they are not interested in. Within your teams and the organization more broadly, you can help leaders think through this dynamic and talk to people about the work they will be engaged in prior to asking if they would like to be part of the team. "Voluntelling" people to be on teams is not a great practice. Asking people if they might be interested and outlining the importance of the work and the benefits of the work are far more effective practices for populating teams.

The importance of tzhe work can be framed to generate interest in terms of how the work:

- Broadly helps the organization achieve its goals
- Complements the individual's goals and aspirations
- Helps the individual develop new skills
- Helps the individual develop new networks and contacts

Purposefully thinking through how you can appeal to prospective team members in ways that intersect with what they might be interested in allows people to come into the team with a positive perspective. In doing so, you demonstrate that you care enough about their opinion to take the time to talk to and recruit them rather than voluntelling. There is an enormous difference in the two approaches, one that broadcasts to the prospect how they might be treated, respected, and valued on the team.

In other words, there is a coercive quality to voluntelling people to be on teams. There is a hint of disrespect and dishonesty in it, because it intimates that you don't care enough about the prospective team member's opinion, and even dignity, to actually put in the effort of framing the work in a way that will appeal to them. This dynamic tells prospects a great deal about how they will be treated on the team. They may go along with being told to be on the team, but will enter the group with doubt, mistrust, and low engagement.

This intersects with trust and honesty. Recruiting is your first opportunity to demonstrate how you will treat members of your team. People will ask themselves, "Will I be respected? Will I be valued? Will my opinions and perspectives be heard? And importantly, will my leader be honest with me?" Telling versus asking demonstrates a great deal about how people should feel about the answers to those questions. As such, you should:

- Dedicate yourself to being honest with the team about the value of the work—its importance, the motivations for the work, constraints upon the work, and the scope of the work.
- Create an individual recruitment strategy for each team member to appeal to what they might find important about being involved in the work and on the team.
- Have a recruiting conversation with prospective team members to gauge their interest and explain their value to the team.

 Consider This

- Be honest with prospective team members about the important work.
- Never voluntell people to be on teams. If they are not interested in the work, then they probably should not be on the team. Engaging people who are disinterested just sets you up for problems. You will have to actively manage these individuals and the potential drag they may have on your team's performance.
- Actively recruit people to the team. Gauge their interest and outline the importance of the work—to the organization and to them. Sell them on why being on the team will be a good use of their talent and time. This is honest behavior and sets up your team for success.

In addition, you can help organization leaders recognize the importance of these activities and work through what those conversations should look like. These recruitment activities will go a long way toward building goodwill with prospects, helping to ensure their interest and engagement, and indicating the way the leader and team will operate going forward.

Regulating Stress

To create the circumstances whereby team trust and psychological safety emerge, it is important for you to effectively manage and leverage stress among the team. In this context, stress can be a force for good. When teams are not effectively stressed, their journey to trust and the sense of community that great teams share is inhibited and delayed. This may not be intuitive, but teams respond to appropriate levels of stress in the same way that people respond to exercise. When we rigorously work out, we are stressing our body. The body responds by building greater muscle mass and cardiovascular capacity in response to that stress. In effect, rigorous exercise damages the body and, in its effort to repair that damage, the body grows its capacity.

Similarly, when teams are subjected to appropriate stress, they respond by building greater team capacity. Teams quickly begin to figure out who does what best, how to effectively distribute work, how to leverage conflict, and how to formulate coping strategies to support one another. The key here is for you to ensure that teams, in effect, suffer injury but not permanent harm.

Effectively regulating this kind of injury is the key to moving teams more quickly to performance. And this is also why it is important to create a team where the efforts of each team member are required to successfully engage with the important work. When there are too many team members, work is less evenly distributed and the efforts of all are not necessarily required. In such a case, the team is not appropriately stressed.

I once consulted with the leader of an L&D department whose team was struggling with the creation of an enterprise inclusion program. Susan was a young and relatively new department head, and this was her first experience with a cross-functional team working on an enterprise initiative. She was convinced her team was not working effectively.

When we spoke, her frustration was obvious. "Timelines are lagging, team members are not showing up, and work quality is not where it should be," she said. "I need the team to engage with this project and I need them to be at least sort of self-directing."

After some diagnostic questions, it was clear that she had made the up-front effort to ensure that the work was properly framed in its importance. But the timeline showed that she had extended due dates and deliverables far into the future. I asked her about this.

She was quick to answer with some pride at what she thought was good leadership acumen. She said, "Well, everyone is working on a number of other projects and I was trying to be cool with the team by making sure that the work they had to do did not stress them too much. I want them to be interested in this project, not annoyed by it."

This was a mistake. By extending timelines too far into the future, the team thought that they had plenty of time to get the work done. There was little urgency on the team to solve problems and do the hard work that success required. The team had become used to putting things off until the next meeting and generally kicking the can down the road. They were, in essence, allowed to not fully engage with the work and with each other. In an effort to be a considerate team leader, she had unwittingly sown the seeds for the team's failure.

In working through the issue, we talked about strategies she could employ to resurrect the team. At first, she suggested bringing the team together and having them figure out the way forward. This might engage the team and give them some autonomy in determining their path. While the timelines and deliverables suggested that the work might not be all that important, it actually was. And it was important enough that it needed to be finished by the due date. At the current trajectory, the team was in danger of not meeting their deliverables. The "slack" she gave the team was endangering the deliverable deadline.

Susan ended up bringing the team together, reiterating the importance of the work and the due date. She outlined her observations and dissatisfaction with team performance, and moved up deliverables and timelines. She also, and most controversially, required the team to come in the following Saturday to complete the design phase of the project and figure out how to meet new deadlines.

To reset the team, she used her positional power to place them in some amount of discomfort, thereby reiterating the importance of the work. The stress forced the team to coordinate and cooperate to figure out how they would meet new deadlines despite the other work they had. She was careful not to make new deadlines unrealistic. Rather, she made the dates a stretch: achievable but difficult, the correct amount of discomfort. This would force the team to begin more fully relying on one another, and also give them the opportunity to fulfill their duty to each other and to the work. It is important to note that she also showed up on that Saturday, demonstrating her commitment to the work and to the team. She suffered right along with them.

Her efforts worked very well. As you can imagine, after some inevitable grumbling, the team figured out new timelines, learned to rely on one another, developed higher levels of trust, and shared equally in the effort. Her calculated strategy to place the team under stress began to provide the circumstances whereby the team suffered together so they could begin to build the kind of trust and vulnerability that great teams demonstrate.

Rather than looking at stress as something to be avoided, you should use and regulate it so teams can develop team skills. Team builds do not have the power to do this. Only hard, important work has the power to mold high-performing teams. You should design team deliverables and due dates with this in mind. In this light, stress regulation is an important part of building team trust and cohesion.

Consider This

- Trust is generated through shared struggle in accomplishing important work. When teams do not have to struggle, they may not generate high levels of trust. They may not be forced to be exactly who they are, and to be valued for it.
- Stress forces the team to adapt, overcome, and build team cohesion and muscle.
- Ensure that the team is sized such that the effort of every team member is required. Ensure that timelines key the team into the importance of the work, and that they are stretched to meet deadlines. Teams will be forced to work together to figure out how to accomplish the goal, and in so doing, will have to rely on one another and see the value that they bring to the success of the team.

Conclusion

It is in doing the work, the struggles that we commonly share, and the act of being trustworthy through those struggles, when common trust across the team is formed. Trust is the outcome, not a prerequisite. No amount of team builds or other games of the sort can accomplish this. The struggle itself unmasks us and forces us to reveal who we actually are. And as we succeed together, we are valued despite our flaws. Each person becomes a valuable member of a winning team. The sense of community that develops out of that struggle and the trust that forms between team members is what ends up being far more valuable than solving the challenge the team was designed to pursue. It lives on long after the team is disbanded and continues to drive high levels of organizational engagement.

CHAPTER 9

Establish Community and Duty

Once again, we are brought back to our discussion about the value of community, belonging, and purpose. It is a discussion that reiterates something we all already know: Humans are built for teaming, for collaborating, and for cooperating with one another to accomplish important things. And it is in this effort that communities form and flourish. In the end, that is the real goal of teaming: to establish community.

Community represents the bonds that come to us through shared struggle. It springs from the sense of duty and fealty that we feel toward our teammates, reminding us that we cannot let our teammates down. And it is these feelings that drive our most extravagant efforts. Not our fealty to the work. Not our fealty to a set of numbers. But rather our fealty to the people we care about.

I once watched a documentary on World War I where they puzzled over how those men could muster up the courage to rise out of the trenches and charge across open fields in the face of machine gun and artillery fire. How could they keep going forth even after seeing their friends torn to pieces before their eyes? In the documentary they read excerpts from numerous letters that those young soldiers wrote home describing their fears. When talking about the job they had to do, most mentioned not only about how scared they were, but also how afraid they were of letting their comrades down. In the end it was fear of failing their team that drove them over the top of the trench and into hell, not their duty to take the trench from the enemy. Soldiers from all wars talk about how, in the end, they fought more for each other than the mission.

This is an extreme example, but an instructive one. You will get some amount of discretionary effort and engagement from people as they seek to fulfill their job roles or accomplish one task or another. And this is often enough to keep the machine going and the trains running on time. But the duty and fealty to one another that struggling to accomplish truly important work engenders offers us much more, and the impact goes far beyond the team itself. Such communal feelings extend past the end of a team's engagement. The relationships developed and shared within the team extend across the organization as team members move on to other teams and other roles. The sense of shared community continues to enrich the organization's ability to solve problems.

When communities are formed, we have a duty to them and to each other. We have a duty to fulfill our commitments, to tell the truth, and to help and care for one another. Given that teams are simply small communities of people doing important work together, our duty to our team is no different. The duty we feel on teams engaged in important work drives us to care about each other as much as we care about the goals we are trying to achieve. This is the end-state organizations and team members are seeking when they think of being on a great team. It is not just the creation of products, it is the sense of pride and victory borne from struggle, and the deep bonds that form because of that struggle. It is the feeling that on the team we can be just as we are, and that it is enough; indeed, it is more than enough. It is the feeling that we are valuable, accepted, and loved. And when we love, and are loved in return, our most extravagant efforts to pull each other across the finish line reveal themselves. Not because we are dedicated to a set of numbers, or KPIs, or profit, but because real high-performing teams succeed together. The true power of teams for organizations lies here.

This is truly what this book is about. Important work drives people to struggle together. And it is in that struggle that trust and community are formed.

Leaving Your Ego at the Door and Giving Away All the Credit

Pride and ego are such pernicious things. In my experience, they are the primary inhibitors of team performance and the creation of community. All it takes is one person who is more interested in their own advancement or in being the smartest person in the room to derail the team's potential. I am sure we've all had people like that on our teams, and we can all easily see the toxic effects of such people.

It is the responsibility of team leaders and team members alike to be intolerant of such behaviors and motivations. As such, you need to ensure that you think very carefully about who you put on your teams. Is the prospective team member ambitious to the point to toxicity? Do they always have to be right? Don't select those people. Sure, they may be the kind of person who gets a lot of work done. Those kinds of people often are. But their negative contribution very often outweighs whatever positives they bring in terms of output. The interesting thing is that everyone knows who these people are. And yet we still place them on our teams.

People who demonstrate these kinds of toxic behaviors are generally placed on teams because they get a lot of stuff done and have a significant contribution to make. People highly interested in their advancement are often ambitious and are eager to crank out a lot of work. And "know it alls" often do have considerable smarts to back up the high opinion they have of themselves. But that is not how teams work. For the same reason that all-star teams often lose to regular teams in exhibition matches, the sum of a team's parts is more effective than the individuals that compose it.

When a team is well-functioning and made up of the correct mix of people, it is often more effective than a group of all-star individuals who do not act as a team. This is an obvious truth. And yet we often do not consider this truth when building our teams. We don't take the time to weed out people who are not team players and who will not sublimate their desires for the good of the team and the good of the important work. Slow down and think purposefully about team selection as it pertains to building team community. The objective is not to fill the team with the most knowledgeable subject matter experts or those who can crank out the most work. Rather, the objective is to fill it with people who know how to accomplish the task, and can also effectively function on a team.

In team selection, look for members who have the requisite knowledge but also give praise freely, do not seek all the credit, are not boastful, are highly interested in the work and the goal, and have a high degree of emotional intelligence. Resist the urge to automatically select the boastful over-achiever just because of how much they can accomplish. A well-formed and well-led team, energized by important work, will outperform a team populated with overly ambitious credit-seekers.

Building a Culture of Appreciation

This is not to say that team members do not want to be valued or get praise and credit. What everyone really wants, for the most part, is to be a valuable member of a winning team. The best teams I have been a part of give praise freely. They look for ways to recognize each other. They want to publicly appreciate the work and contributions other team members provide. And this makes sense. When teams have struggled together to accomplish important work, and they develop a sense of community and care that such joint suffering provides, they naturally wish for everyone to succeed. They actually care about one another. When one cares for someone, they want them to know they are appreciated, they want them to know that they are a valuable member of the team. The best teams create these cultures of appreciation.

A culture of appreciation naturally begins to form when teams struggle together to accomplish important work. The development of team community provides the impetus for this. But this is not to say that we cannot build such a culture into the value system of our team from the beginning. You can set the example by offering sincere and public praise to team members who not only do great work, but also exhibit the characteristics of great team players. This praise not only amounts to a reward for those team members, but also sets an example for the rest of the team. They'll begin to see that praise itself is a rewarded behavior. The end-state is to move the team into creating an appreciation culture.

For the teams you're on, leave your ego at the door and contribute to a culture of appreciation. Commit to the success of the team and your team members, not just to yourself. It can be frustrating to be on a team and not get the appropriate amount of praise and recognition for the work you do. I often coach people who wish to receive praise to instead offer it to others—to give away all the credit. Consistently be on the lookout for people who are doing good things and offer them praise both publicly and privately. This not only offers the team an example of the power of consistent praise, but it also helps orient the team towards a culture of appreciation. Incidentally, it will likely begin to remove your frustration as well when you, in turn, begin to get praise from others.

I have also noticed that leaders are sometimes reticent to publicly praise individual team members. Often, they resort to broad statements of praise for the team. In coaching leaders and probing to understand this dynamic, I have found that many leaders do not want to diminish the con-tributions of others by singling out an individual for praise. I understand this thought, but the assumption that it is built on is incorrect.

Praise is not a zero-sum game in which one person's praise comes at the cost of another. In a high-performing team, there is plenty of praise to go around. In teams that have not reached the high-performing phase, praise is a reward that orients people to what is valued. As such, people on the team will begin to reorient their efforts in ways that will garner praise. What is rewarded is where people will spend their time and effort. And inversely, people avoid what is punished. You should look for opportunities to offer individual praise often and be sure that it aligns with the behaviors you'd like to encourage in others.

An appreciation culture is what you are trying to create. And what you praise is significant. Praising that which helps the team accomplish its goals, and thereby driving behaviors that are valuable, begins to shape your culture. However, it is important to note that you must only praise that which is actually valuable—don't praise people for merely coming to work. That diminishes the value of praise. When we stand up and say, "I'd like to thank Amal for showing up today," that is clearly silly. And yet, in an effort to build an appreciation culture, that is the kind of thing I sometimes see. Don't do this. Reserve your praise for meaningful contributions to the valuable work. This means that you must always be on the lookout for real value when you see it, and you must never let it go unthanked.

 Consider This

- Great teams become a community.
- Communities are formed when people struggle together to accomplish important things. The relationships that communities build together live long after the team is disbanded, and improve the function of your organization.
- Always look for people doing things right and praise them.

Instilling Team Values and Norms

Organizations that lack a common set of values and norms cannot flourish. Big or small, from countries to companies to families, any group of people working together to accomplish something important cannot thrive unless they have an agreed upon set of values, beliefs, and behaviors. Groups need to operate from the same playbook when thinking about what they believe, and what behaviors will be rewarded or punished. In other words, the values and norms we adopt—essentially what we believe in and how we will act—inform us of what we believe is right and what is wrong. And that group mental model leads us to discern what behaviors to adopt.

Values and norms let team members know how they should comport themselves. They can be anything really, as long as the group agrees on them. Typical examples include "we strive for excellence in everything we do" or "we do not let great get in the way of good." These are instructive because they show us that universal values and norms beyond obvious ones like "we don't beat people" or "we don't insult one another's family members."

A team can just as easily adopt a value that says "everything we do will be done at the highest level of excellence" as one that says "we will modulate our work effort to match its importance." Those are both equally valid and yet very different. And teams have the leeway to select which values and norms they find most helpful to whatever they are trying to accomplish.

When team members do not operate from the same values, norms, and behaviors, they are not operating from the same playbook. And one can easily see how this is suboptimal. If some members are working toward the highest degree of excellence while others believe that good enough is good enough, the two groups will be at odds. One group will be frustrated that the other are lazy shirkers while the other group will be frustrated that the first group's level of effort is wasting valuable time and resources. High-functioning teams develop a set of beliefs on how they will operate to most effectively drive the team to accomplish the important work that they all agree on.

Leaders often do not pay nearly enough attention to this during the beginning phases of team formation. Or if they do, it is often only lip-service. Team values are too often quickly forgotten and never brought up again. This is a critical area in which you can contract with your teams to create mutually agreed-upon values and norms, and build processes to keep them alive.

The dangerous truth is that if you do not purposefully develop the values and norms your team will adopt, a set of values and norms will evolve for you. And those values and norms could very well be less effective in helping you solve the important problems that your team is engaged with. All kinds of pathologies can develop when teams do not purposefully design their culture.

For example, strong personalities that are vying for influence or display other toxic behaviors can easily run roughshod over other team members. A team norm to ignore this behavior rather than confront it head on can quickly develop. The team may then develop time-consuming and potentially morale-reducing behaviors to accommodate the toxic behavior rather than dealing with it. Instead, the purposeful introduction of team norms and accompanying processes that minimize such behaviors can go a long way to reducing the toxic impact of such individuals. The team might align on a value that says "everyone gets input into decisions or discussions" and an accompanying process that says, "each member will be required to voice their perspective during decision points."

To be fair, important work often drives groups to organically evolve norms that work. If team members are dedicated to the important work, they naturally wish to be successful. That belief drives the team to evolve behaviors that work and discard those that do not. However, the trial and error associated with that kind of behavioral evolution is time consuming. It's far better to purposefully work through a base set of values and norms that the team can get behind up front. As they work together, they will naturally modify, revise, and evolve them into even more effective values and norms.

Well-functioning groups not only develop a set of beliefs and values that they agree upon, they also develop mechanisms to enforce those beliefs and values. In high-functioning teams, members hold each other accountable to the agreed-upon set of beliefs, norms, and behaviors. And again, we are reminded of the importance of important work. Important work is helpful in prompting team members to call out toxic or ineffective norms and behaviors. The less important the work, the more likely people will disengage and become apathetic to suboptimal team behaviors. Important work drives conflict and encourages team members to challenge one another.

You can help the team to purposefully design team norms and behaviors, and then ask the team to hold one another accountable to them. You can, and should, require the team to hold them accountable as a model for how they should hold each other accountable. You should state, "Here are my values and I am asking you to hold me accountable to them."

An easy example is a team norm that says, "We are on time for our meetings." If you are late to a meeting, and if no one calls you out on it, you should ask the team why they didn't call you out. In fact, you should require that they do so. And when a team member does call you out, you should publicly praise them for doing so. In this way, the team is given a model of how to drive accountability. The praise garnered from engaging in that accountability telegraphs that it is a worthwhile behavior.

Leveraging Teaming as Development

This may seem obvious, but time and again I see team selection based on who can do the work rather than who needs to do the work. Teaming has the potential to be one of the more significant developmental experiences that you have at your disposal. And yet, in the urge to get things done quickly and effectively, we are often drawn to selecting team members who have the technical expertise to quickly and effectively get the work done. Depending on the criticality of the work, this is sometimes the right call. But more often than not, we do have sufficient time to select a team that has a good mix of technical expertise and those who could greatly benefit in terms of their development. This purposeful selection of experience and development need gives more experienced people on the team the opportunity to develop the less experienced. The close working relationships that evolve on effective teams allow less experienced people to dig in and get their hands dirty. This allows them to build experience with the backstop of seasoned mentors to help ensure their success. The struggles, successes, and failures of the team then become the successes and failures of the novice. This kind of development is invaluable not only in terms of developing technical skill, but also in navigating the broader organization, building and harnessing cross-functional relationships, and developing leadership skills. Up-and-coming leaders can learn about aligning the team, communicating priorities, and generally upskilling their leadership.

Purposefully building a team to develop people in the organization also builds your talent bench strength. Teams are often made up of the same people time after time. These go-to people often become burned out by being selected for every team you have. Developing people through teams can help ensure that you have a variety of people to choose from. This reduces burnout among the go-to people and additionally builds higher levels of engagement across your group as people engage in purposeful development activities.

Teams are not only great vehicles for leader and individual development, but they are also a great venue to watch how people perform on a team. You can observe how individuals cooperate and collaborate, how they challenge, and whether they can sublimate themselves to the good of the team and the work. Observing people struggle with a team to accomplish important work is an excellent way to see how they really are. People's true colors begin to show rather quickly, and with this information we can get good insight into whether they behave in ways that are selfish, arrogant, ambitious to the point of toxicity, or other ways that are damaging for the team. If your organization has a defined set of values and ways in which people in the organization should comport themselves (and you certainly should), it quickly becomes clear who will live by these values. These observations can help inform us as to who we should consider for promotions and development, or even consider excising from the organization.

You can play an important role here. If one of TD's primary roles is to be the conscience of the organization and an influencer of values, culture, and behaviors, then their input on team selection and observations of team member behaviors can help to ensure teams are populated with the kind of people the organization needs to keep and grow. You should work closely with leaders to convey their observations of team member effectiveness as it pertains to teaming behaviors. Leaders can then adjust to coach negative behaviors or remove team members as needed. They can also consider that behavior when considering promotion decisions.

Embracing Diversity in Team Makeup

When you begin to think about building out a team, you should absolutely include diverse perspectives and experiences. Having the same kind of people populate a team often leads to the same ideas and solutions. Select people who not only have diverse experiences and perspectives, but also diverse ways of thinking, working, and collaborating. There is no hard and fast rule for how many of each kind of person you might have, but you should think about the different personalities, perspectives, and organizational stakeholders who will be affected by whatever initiative you are working on.

Some people are focused on getting stuff done, some people like to think about stuff, some people are talkative, and others are taciturn. Some people are focused on other people and others are focused on the process itself. All these personalities and styles are important on a team. In working with and observing teams over the years, I have seen this play out over and over and I have concluded that, depending on how time-sensitive the work is, the most effective solutions are generated when different kinds of people are working on a problem.

As you develop a team, you should think about populating it with what I call offsetting personalities. These are people whose tendencies offset one another to arrive at a middle ground that most effectively functions. Action-oriented versus data driven, tried and true versus innovative, people-oriented versus process-oriented. These opposite perspectives tend to offset, or moderate, one another so that the team doesn't either jump the gun or languish in analysis paralysis. There are obviously a million ways to slice and dice perspectives and personalities, but the point here is to be purposeful in the selection of a team so that it has different kinds of people who can look at the problem and solve it from multiple perspectives.

In working with a leader of an HR group to build a team of consultants tasked with creating a major culture change initiative, I encouraged the leader to think about populating the team in just this way. We worked through facets of personality and experience to ensure that the team had the correct mix. She purposefully sat down with pen and paper and scratched out the personality, technical, and experience characteristics she thought would make for the best team possible. The team was to be composed of five people. She immediately selected an individual who she knew to have the requisite technical and organizational experience to tackle the problem. However, she also knew this individual was highly data driven and relatively indecisive. She therefore selected another individual who, while lacking in some technical skills related to the problem statement, was very organized and decisive and would help to keep the team on track. A third individual was selected to provide, in her terms, "wild and innovative ideas" that would challenge the team to think broadly about novel ways to approach the problem. The fourth individual was a young but very capable person who would bring energy and enthusiasm, and would greatly benefit from being on the team in terms of learning different aspects of the organization and the challenges it faced. Team membership for this individual would be developmental in nature. Finally, she selected an individual who was a subject matter expert on the issues at hand, and had a very long history with the organization. This individual could leverage their knowledge, relationships, and connections to smooth the way for the team's progress. The leader's selections were purposeful, and she was careful to select people who not only had the skills required to solve the problem, but whose approaches, experience, and personalities effectively complemented one another.

This all may seem obvious. But time and again I see leaders fail to take the time to really think through who should be on the team and who needs to be on the team. Teams are all too often thrown together with little thought beyond who has the technical ability to solve the problem. This does the team a disservice by building a team that does not have complementary skills and perspectives, but it also does the work a disservice. The outcomes will be poorer and less likely to solve the problem. If the work is important, it behooves us to take the time to build a team that has the best possible chance of success. Honor the importance of the work and purposefully select a diverse team.

A word of caution: Selecting different kinds of people is often annoying to people. And why shouldn't it be? We like to surround ourselves with people who are like us. For example, action-oriented people are often frustrated by people who continually need more data before making a decision. We have a tendency to select people who are most like us because it is comfortable. We select people who think like us because we intrinsically tend to trust their judgement more than we trust the judgement of those different from us; the logician distrusts the intuitive. It is one thing to talk about populating teams with different kinds of people in the abstract; it is quite another to actually work with people who annoy us. This is the value and beauty of a curiosity culture built around important work. When we approach those whose methodologies and approaches annoy us, if we are genuinely curious in the service of important work, we may begin to glean some value from them and the way they go about their business. Implementation of "tell me more" and the interview format provides a template to engage in the kind of curious discourse that can lead to greater understanding. It helps us see the value in perspectives that we may initially find less valuable.

I will concede that integrating different kinds of people into teams does take longer. In time-sensitive and critical situations, it may be better to stack your team with those who have the requisite technical knowledge, and who can quickly integrate into an effective unit to accomplish a short turnaround task. For example, during the 2020 pandemic, I worked with a technology group that had to quickly come up with a remote work plan and develop ad hoc supporting technology platforms to ensure immediate business continuity. A hit team was put together with a turnaround time measured in days. The thinking around assembling that team was less about integrating different perspectives and more about how quickly they could get something up and running. This, of course, happens, but it is definitely not the rule. The vast majority of teams I have worked with have sufficient time to meaningfully build out a diverse group.

Consider This

- Teams that do not have a common set of values and norms are less effective.
- It is better to proactively align on common values and norms in the early stages of team creation. If you don't purposefully align on values and norms, the team may align on something less effective.
- Model the agreed-on values and norms and require the team to hold you accountable.

Conclusion

Teams that do not have a shared sense of how they will act, interact, and comport themselves are much less likely to become high-performing teams and create the trust and community that great teams have. Teams, or any group for that matter, that do not have a shared understanding of what they believe, what their values are, and what their norms are will waste a lot of energy in trying to figure out how to most effectively cooperate and collaborate. Toxic behaviors can easily creep into team dynamics and derail forward momentum as the team tries to figure out how to work around them. Purposefully aligning on team values and norms up front and actively building processes to drive the team to hold one another accountable will go a long way to building a team culture that is effective. You can, and should, model such behavior and model holding each other accountable by requiring the team to hold them accountable.

CHAPTER 10
Putting It All Together

Teams are powerful things, and well they should be. They are the mechanism that has propelled humanity forward for thousands of years. Important work brings out the best in people. And inversely, unimportant work tends to bring out the worst. Leveraging the power for creation and community that important work provides is the most critical thing that you or any organization, no matter how large, can do. It propels us to our most extravagant efforts to not only accomplish the work itself, but also care for and hold up those who accompany us on that journey. Teams engaged in important work allow organizations and people to flourish in ways great and small. And the connections forged during the shared struggle of teams permeate the organization long after the team has disbanded.

We do not often think much about creating the circumstances necessary for teams to thrive in this way, and that is too bad. We lose huge opportunities by giving short shrift to how we assemble and orient our teams. When done well, they have the power to elevate and validate. When done poorly, they have the power to diminish and destroy. I often wonder at the opportunity cost of this. How much do organizations lose in terms of talent and engagement when they do not pay sufficient attention to the very thing that has the most power to shape the organization? Teams have the power to shape their successes and failures, and provide people with the sense that they are valuable and worthy, despite their flaws—indeed, sometimes because of their flaws.

We have talked at length about the criticality of important work and assembling diverse teams with the autonomy to solve problems. We've discussed how teams can most effectively accomplish their goals by engaging in strong challenge through a lens of curiosity. And we've seen how these things can create trust, belonging, and community—the very things that we all need beyond pay or promotion. The very things that, in the end, drive even greater levels of engagement. They create a virtuous cycle that helps not only the organization, but people themselves.

It is my hope that those who have read this far now have the tools, or at least the perspective, to return to your organizations and advocate for giving teaming the purposeful attention it deserves; to effectively clarify important work and craft teams in ways that not only fulfill the needs of the organization, but also of the people who are on them. The benefits in shaping your culture and in providing purpose will grow your organization in ways you may not even imagine.

Index

Page numbers followed by *f* refer to figures.

About the Author

Thane Bellomo is an executive coach and team and organization development practitioner. He has more than 20 years of experience working with Fortune 50 leaders to maximize their potential and optimize their results. Thane is an accomplished author, speaker, and coach and spends his time studying how leaders and teams most effectively form and function. He lives in Harrisburg, Pennsylvania, and can be reached at thanebellomo.com.